ACTION
SPEAKS
LOUDER

P9-BHZ-153

ACTION SPEAKS LOUDER

A Handbook of Nonverbal Group Techniques

A. Jane Remocker MBAOT

Formerly Sole Charge Occupational Therapist, Greater Vancouver Mental Health Service

Elizabeth T. Storch BA OTReg(C)

Formerly Senior Occupational Therapist, Psychiatric Ward, Shaughnessy Hospital

Foreword by J. C. A. Morrant

MB BS D(Obst) RCOG DPM FRCP(C)
Director, Hospital Psychiatric Consultation Service,
Shaughnessy Hospital

Second Edition

CHURCHILL LIVINGSTONE
EDINBURGH LONDON AND NEW YORK 1979

CHURCHILL LIVINGSTONE
Medical Division of Longman Group Limited

Distributed in the United States of America by
Churchill Livingstone Inc., 19 West 44th Street, New York, N.Y. 10036,
and by associated companies, branches and representatives
throughout the world.

First edition 1977
Second edition 1979

ISBN 0 443 01919 3

British Library Cataloguing in Publication Data
Remocker, A Jane
  Action speaks louder. – 2nd ed.
  1. Group psychotherapy 2. Nonverbal
  communication (Psychology)
  I. Title   II. Storch, Elizabeth T
  616.8'915   RC488   79–40259

Printed in Singapore by Kua Co., Book Manufacturer, Pte Ltd.

Foreword

Psychiatrists are a doleful lot. This may be from temperament or arise from the sort of work they tackle. One day I was having lunch with some psychiatric colleagues. As we moodily poked at our tunafish salad, we asked each other how we coped with those periods of despondency which most of us seem heir to. We agreed that to *do* something dispels gloom most rapidly. Painting a fence, mowing the lawn, building a canoe, romping with the children, shucking peas, all help. This book is about doing things.

This book is about more than just doing things. It is about doing things with *people*. The anxieties and heartaches of this life are almost always associated with the way we interact with our fellows. Although, over the tunafish salad, we praised the healing powers of action, by the time the coffee arrived, we agreed that *words* are important, too.

This book describes many techniques which pivot around speech. It is a lie that, 'Sticks and stones can break your bones, words can never hurt you.' Words can hurt one, and they can encourage ('. . . we're behind you . . .'), delight ('I love you . . .'), warm ('. . . you can be vexing, but we're still very fond of you . . .'), and so on.

This book describes a large number of well-tried exercises for small groups, exercises devised and refined by the book's experienced authors. The group activities, which are explained and can be easily imitated, are designed to assist clients relate to other people in more appropriate, wholesome and rewarding ways. The activities described range from ice-breakers, to more sophisticated processes to help a person understand himself or herself better; how he or she affects others, and is affected by others.

What I like so much about this book is that a lot of it is hugely enjoyable. Losing one's shyness, asserting oneself, liking oneself and people better, need not always be full of tears and tension. Healthy changing can be fun and sometimes hilarious, as this book shows. Try it and see.

J.C.A.M.

ABOUT THE AUTHORS

A. Jane Remocker is a graduate of the Dorset House School of Occupational Therapy, Oxford, England. She has eight years' experience working in a variety of psychiatric settings. She has been responsible for setting up programs in an acute-care hospital and a day-care program and is widely experienced in working with groups of chronic psychiatric patients. She served as a consultant to community based organizations working with psychiatric patients.

Elizabeth T. Storch obtained her BA at the University of British Columbia and is a graduate of the Kingston School of Occupational Therapy, Ontario, Canada. During her thirteen years of clinical experience she has gained a reputation for being an expert in group techniques with psychiatric patients. She has acted as a consultant in nonverbal techniques for both acute and chronic patients, and has been a guest lecturer at the School of Rehabilitation Medicine, University of British Columbia.

Preface

Occupational therapy and its application has undergone some radical changes in the last few years. In the field of psychiatry there has also been a definite move towards the realization that it is often more effective to expose people to the advantages of group therapy (as opposed to individual treatment) as well as to provide them with the practical skills that will be essential to them when they leave the treatment setting. This has meant that a book such as *Action Speaks Louder* has been welcomed by both occupational therapists and other professionals.

Action Speaks Louder evolved as the result of our clinical work in an acute-care psychiatric teaching hospital. There we frequently found ourselves in the situation of advising other professionals and students about techniques to use with groups of more severely disturbed patients. Not only were we consulted for our ideas but also for the therapeutic potential of them. The demand was such that eventually it became expedient to write the techniques down and collect them together in sections that focused on certain specific problem areas that patients frequently needed assistance with. It was also apparent that the instructions had to be clear and simple, since those using them came from a variety of professional backgrounds and had very varying amounts of clinical experience.

Obviously there was a need for a book such as *Action Speaks Louder* but, because it was rather unusual, we were unable to prove its marketability to publishers. However, we believed so strongly in it that we decided to take the risk of printing and distributing the book ourselves. We were rewarded by a very enthusiastic response from both individuals and universities and, as a result of this, were offered the opportunity to have *Action Speaks Louder* published by Churchill Livingstone of Edinburgh. This, perhaps, sums up the brief history of our book and explains why, only a year after bringing it onto the market, we are introducing a second edition.

Action Speaks Louder was written as a convenient reference book for occupational therapists, registered and psychiatric nurses, social workers, psychologists, teachers and clergymen, as well as for anyone else who finds themselves working with people who are experiencing severe emotional problems. Because of its unusual layout and clear instructions, the application of nonverbal group techniques may appear very simple, but be aware that becoming a successful group leader will only come with practice. Therefore, we cannot stress too much that the experiential learning of group techniques and their application is most important, since there is nothing that can replace personal training under the guidance of people more experienced than oneself. The dynamics of being in a group and the power of working closely with other people makes one more sensitive to the application of techniques and their potential.

In the second edition of this book we have expanded the glossary to be more comprehensive and enlarged the bibliography to include some of the most recent publications. We have been grateful for this opportunity to update our book and hope it will fulfil its purpose and provide you, the reader, with considerable enjoyment.

Vancouver, 1979   A.J.R.
                                                                                                                  E.T.S.

Acknowledgements

The set of concepts developed while working in a profession originate from many sources and from contact with many people. Thus it would be an impossible task to identify every person who has contributed to this book and it is probable that some would not even recognize their contribution. There are, however, a few people who have played a significant part in helping bring *Action Speaks Louder* to completion.

Mrs Shirley Salomon spent a great deal of time editing and evaluating the original manuscript. Her enthusiasm was invaluable, while her wisdom and analytical skills enabled her to suggest some constructive changes. Dr J. C. A. Morrant, with whom we have both worked, recognized the value of structured nonverbal exercises with chronic psychiatric patients and encouraged us to continue developing and refining them. Ken Buhay and his co-workers in Encountering Theatre taught us how to be uninhibited and introduce laughter, spontaneity and fantasy into therapeutic groups by using a wide variety of theatre games.

Lastly, we are indebted to all those patients with whom we have worked. Without their participation and enthusiasm this book could not have been written.

Contents

Introduction

In this manual you will find a collection of exercises which have been designed to help an individual discover himself and his feelings. The self-awareness which he will gain will give him the strength to go out and not only meet other people but also experience true communication with them.

The exercises have come to us as folk-songs come to the balladeer. Some of them have been handed down from person to person and as a result, have become changed. They are described as variations and appear as footnotes to the original exercises. Some exercises have been invented in order to solve a particular problem at hand and some have developed spontaneously from a previous exercise or from one aspect of a group's discussion.

We have compiled this book of techniques as a result of our own experiences working with small groups of patients in a variety of psychiatric settings. These people, aside from their presenting problems, often seemed to exhibit one or more of the following general difficulties:

— inability to communicate effectively with others
— inability to recognize and express their feelings
— inability to perceive others and/or self accurately
— inability to generate more than an inadequate and limited number of solutions to personal problems
— inability to control the arousal of debilitating anxiety

Because of these difficulties these patients could not be included in a *verbal* group and yet they too needed the opportunity to identify and talk about their problems. We found that, if we could present these people with the means of expressing themselves through some form of action, this was not only less threatening but also gave them a recent and real experience to talk about. We have come to realize, since we began using these exercises, that this mode of working has a far wider application than the chronic patients with whom we began. This is because the exercises provide an opportunity for learning, learning new and more appropriate ways of relating, learning about oneself and one's reactions to situations, and learning about other people. The key to their effectiveness, however, is that they are simple and enjoyable for the participants. Although the exercises are written in a form that is suitable for use with chronic patients, they can be adapted to suit the age, level of functioning and purpose of any group of people who meet together in order to improve their self-awareness and ability to interact.

The book contains fifty exercises, representing various forms of creative expression. By using these exercises we hope the reader will acquire the philosophy, experience and confidence which is necessary to create new exercises more suited to the specific needs of the reader's own clientele.

In general the exercises fall into three major categories: *Introductory exercises, Active exercises and Verbal exercises*. For easy reference, therefore, they have been grouped in the Index under the following headings: Introductory or Warm-up exercises, Active exercises, Verbal exercises, Projective techniques and Theatre games.

Introductory exercises are techniques which help people who do not know one another to become acquainted. They are usually used at the beginning of a session, but can be introduced at other times if it is appropriate. This category includes the *warm-up* exercises which are techniques of short duration used to promote an atmosphere in which a person can begin to look at specific problems in greater detail.

Active exercises are techniques which tend to promote body awareness, coordination and/or interaction of a nonverbal kind. Generally, the stimulation required to hold the individual's attention is external, provided by the group as a whole or by individuals within it. Since a person's resistance is often well developed when it comes to words, use has been made of various expressive media such as music, art and drama.[1] These forms of creative expression enable a person to say something about himself at a time when he is still unable to express himself in words. Many of the exercises also provide an opportunity for a person to experience situations which he might avoid normally. The exercises enable members to loosen up with more basic instinctual and physical forms of expression such as in body rhythm, movement, or use of colour and may allow them to find new aspects of themselves which they may wish to explore, develop or change.

Verbal exercises are techniques generally of a more intellectual and sedentary nature. They tend to focus on such skills as the ability to speak clearly and concisely, to recall past knowledge and to organize thoughts logically. Many of the exercises make use of words, both written and spoken, and are ways of practising more effective communication. In contrast to the *active exercises* the stimulation required to hold an individual's attention must often come from within himself.

LAYOUT   The manual has been designed as a practical textbook for the student interested in expanding his knowledge of group techniques and as a handy reference book for the graduate therapist or teacher. It has been organized

---

1. The drama exercises included in the text are usually referred to as *Theatre games*. These are simple, structured exercises often used by actors to improve their abilities to think quickly, to be spontaneous, to improvise, to speak clearly, to trust others, to work in cooperation with others, to concentrate and to be decisive. The emphasis in most of them is upon clear, direct communication whether it be verbal or nonverbal, and if they are used well they offer an excellent opportunity to practise, improve or change social behaviour in an enjoyable and accepting atmosphere.

to be read and used as one would a cookery book and the essential ingredients, which should be considered before carrying out the procedure, are listed under the following headings: *Recommended for these problems, Stage of group development* and *Materials and equipment*.

The layout for each exercise is identical and the following is an explanation of the various headings we have used.

Title. This is the descriptive heading which is designed to help the leader quickly recall the technique involved. For example, *Who am I?* is an exercise in self-awareness.

Time. An approximate time allowance is given. This should be of assistance in the planning of a session, since it is important to know whether to use one exercise or several during the time available.

Recommended for these problems. If the exercises in this book are to be constructive and appropriate they should be related specifically to the problems of the people in the group. The first thing to do, therefore, is to identify the problem areas and then choose exercises which relate to them.[2] Several different problem areas can be focused upon in any one exercise.

Stage of group development. Under this heading we have indicated the degree of closeness in relationships which we feel should exist amongst the group members in order for the exercise to be appropriate. Whether an exercise is suitable or not for a particular group of people depends on many complex factors. The general statements we have made regarding suitability, therefore, should be used as a guideline only. However, in deciding whether to use an exercise or not, we feel the amount of interpersonal contact that is required by the exercise and the amount of interpersonal sharing that the group can actually tolerate are very important factors.

Synopsis. Under this heading you will find a thumbnail sketch of the exercise itself, including the goals and means of attaining them. The synopsis is designed with two purposes in mind. Firstly, that you, as the leader, can assess quickly whether the exercise is appropriate and secondly, that once you are familiar with it's title, you can recall the procedure easily.

Materials and equipment. In this section we have listed those things that need to be organized or prepared before starting an exercise. The materials required for some exercises include the preparation of a list of topics. Where this is necessary we have compiled some suggestions and these are found directly after the exercise. The ideal setting has been indicated but this is a guide only.

---

2. In North America many hospitals are computerizing their medical records in such a way that information about the patient, his treatment and progress are recorded in relation to his problems. This method, known as the Problem Oriented Medical Record, is practical and easy to use. A person's problems are identified and then a treatment program is designed which relates specifically to the problem list.

Procedure. This section is divided in half longitudinally. On the left-hand side of the page is a step by step description of how the exercise can be presented. On the right-hand side of the page is an explanation of the therapeutic aspects of some of the steps.

Discussion topics. The discussion which follows participation in any exercise is an important part of the whole experience. In fact, the main purpose of some exercises is merely to stimulate conversation. The discussion time allows a person to talk about his subjective reactions, hear the comments of others and consider how this experience relates to his daily life. Without a discussion, most of the exercises may appear purposeless to the participants and lack relevance to their problems. Under this heading, in each exercise, you will find a few ideas to present to your group members for their consideration.

Comments. We have presented the exercises in their most basic and, therefore, structured format. For this reason they will not be suitable for all situations or all groups of people. The *Comments* space is an opportunity to record personal observations regarding the effectiveness of a particular exercise, variations that could be tried and recommendations for the future.

In reading through the book and in carrying out the exercises described, it should be pointed out that exercises, such as these, will rarely be used in isolation. They are far more likely to be utilized as part of a person's total treatment program which may include such other things as chemotherapy, individual supportive psychotherapy, occupational therapy and recreational activities.

Finally, the book has been written to be used as a practical manual. We anticipate it will give ideas, stimulate the imagination and provide a creative method of approaching problems. However, it is only a beginning. We hope, therefore, that it will provide a firm basis for the reader to develop a larger and more personalized repertoire of exercises.

Some basic concepts

When preparing and leading any kind of group session or class there are many aspects that should be taken into consideration. We would like to use this chapter to share some of the concepts that we have learned as a result of our experience working with groups.

FORETHOUGHTS
Planning a group

It is a mistake to underestimate the devastating effects resulting from insufficient preparation. The group leader should prepare not only the equipment and materials required but, in addition, should give thought to the sequence of exercises or *menu*. Rather like a balanced meal the session should consist of a beginning, middle and end and in order to do this effectively the following points should be considered:

The needs of each person. In any group, each person will have his own particular problems. These become translated into the goals that the person hopes to achieve, or at least work towards, while participating in appropriate exercises.

This is always the first thing to think about, because it makes it possible to choose a *focus* for the session. The *focus* will probably be problem related but where possible should be expressed in positive terms. For example, if one of the problems is that most of the people in the group are afraid of looking at one another then the focus of the session could be *eye-contact*.

We find that a *focus* helps people work on specific problems and also gives them a sense of doing something which is both purposeful and constructive. Too often, particularly in hospitals, patients are involved in groups and required to participate in various activities but no one ever thinks to tell them why they are doing something, or what they might expect to learn from it. So they feel anxious and apprehensive as they leave a session wondering what it was all about.

The level of group cohesiveness. This is quite difficult to ascertain accurately but can be assessed in terms of 'How long has the group been meeting together?', 'How much do the group members relate to one another?', 'How comfortable are they in group situations?', 'Do they trust one another?', 'Do they take an interest in or support one another?', and 'Can they risk expressing their feelings to one another?'.

Consideration of the above questions makes it possible to determine which exercises are suitable, since each exercise varies in the amount of interaction and personal sharing that it requires. For example, if a group is meeting together for the first time, it is unlikely that the people in it will feel able to share their most intimate problems right away. It would be much more suitable to focus the session on *becoming acquainted* and to utilize some exercises which would help the participants do this easily.

3 *The varying levels of concentration*. Every person in a group will be able to concentrate for a different amount of time. Assessing this variable will help determine both which exercises are appropriate and also how many to use. A person's concentration tends to improve if he is truly interested in what is happening and if he is constantly involved and stimulated. This can be achieved if he is active and doing something, rather than sitting and talking, or if he is given a part in the proceedings. Therefore, in a group where the majority of people have difficulty concentrating, it is usually advisable to use several exercises and to choose ones which are active rather than sedentary.

4 *The size of the group*. Obviously this is an important factor because some exercises are more effective when used with a large group of people and some more suited to a small group. For example, many of the *theatre games* require an audience component. Other exercises, such as *Eavesdropping*, would take a long time if the group were large and everyone was to take a turn. We find the optimum size for a therapeutic group is eight to ten people, including staff.

If a group is small, e.g. five people including staff, we have noticed that the participants tend to become anxious and may be reluctant to attend. This is usually because they are unsure of themselves and are afraid of being forced to participate, thereby appearing either a fool or a failure in front of other people. With this size of group, *video-replay techniques* can be used to advantage since there is time available to record, watch the tape and use it as a reference for discussion.[1] It is also possible to adapt and structure an exercise so that it can be done with two or three people just as effectively as with ten.

On the other hand, if a group is very large, then it can be extremely difficult to help the quiet, withdrawn person to become involved. It is sometimes best to split a large group into smaller units, or structure the session so that the quiet members have an opportunity to join in.

5 *Expectations, the group leader's and the participants'*. These play a very important part in any group session and a leader should always be conscious of them. It is appropriate for a group leader to have expectations; but the group leader's expectations should be realistic and not cause anxiety amongst the group members. Whenever possible the expectations of both the leader and participants should be discussed openly, for even if they are not talked about they are sensed and will affect everyone. The other aspect of expectations is that, if they are not met, then they tend to evoke a wide range of feelings. The group leader may feel irritated, angry or disappointed, whilst the group members may experience a sense of failure, inadequacy

---

1. See Section on *Video-replay techniques*, p. 8.

or anxiety. If the expectations of everyone, both the leader and the participants, are clear and explicit, then the format of the session and the experiences gained as a result of it will probably be more positive and rewarding.

Once these five points have been considered, it is possible to put together a program that suits the needs of the individuals who will be participating, reflects the general functioning level of the group and is flexible. The flexibility is vital since it will allow the opportunity for the program to develop in a new or unexpected direction initiated by the participants rather than by the group leader.

Choice of exercises

There is great skill involved in assessing interpersonal problems and strengths and in knowing how to work with them in a group setting. However, there are no hard and fast rules for choosing exercises, so that although some of it can be learned, the rest comes with experience. We recommend trying a particular exercise or combination of exercises. The results may not be what you expect, but if you are prepared to evaluate the outcome afterwards, it will be a worthwhile learning experience for you as the group leader.

In order to plan an effective group session it is as important to know the needs of the group members as it is to know the procedure of the exercise which will be used. With this in mind we have cross-indexed the exercises according to the various problem areas on which they focus.

There are some specific problems that participants may be experiencing which contraindicate the choice of certain exercises. These are:

— incapacitating side-effects of medication on an individual such as tremor, blurred vision, Parkinsonism and dry mouth (contraindicated would be such exercises as *Playreading* and *Simultaneous conversations*)
— individuals with low ego-strength but high I.Q., i.e. those who are demoralized by their diminished ability to think and who feel 'put-down' by being asked to participate in exercises which they feel are simple and childish (contraindicated would be *Body X's & O's* or *Newspaper quiz*)
— the over-active person who is extremely easily stimulated and has a tendency to interrupt or be disruptive (contraindicated would be *Movement and sound circle* or *Soapbox debate*)
— the suspicious person whose suspiciousness may tend to be increased by the nature of the exercise (contraindicated would be *Eavesdropping*)

Always choose exercises which you, yourself, feel confident and comfortable doing, since your own involvement and enthusiasm will tend to inspire the group members. The experience should, in general, be an enjoyable and worthwhile one for everybody involved.

Related exercises

Choosing exercises and combinations of exercises is a skilful task. No matter how far apart the sessions are, they should be structured so that each exercise and session builds on the momentum and gains of the previous exercise or session. Thus it is possible to plan either a daily, weekly or monthly program that serves the needs of the group members and is a sequence of events, focusing on certain specific and identifiable goals. For example, given the general goal *to become acquainted*, a session could commence with a *warm-up* exercise such as the *Name game* and continue with one or two other related exercises such as *Likes and dislikes* or *Introductions*.

Location and time

The next things to consider, when planning a group session, are where it should be held and at what time. The location chosen should be appropriate for the exercises to be used and the time convenient for all concerned. Whatever the location and time chosen, we feel that these two factors should remain consistent throughout the life of the group. Even if one plans to use a different location for a particular session it is far better to meet at the usual location and move on from there. This makes it easier for each person to arrive on time and consider the session as a predictable part of his day. This is particularly true when the participants are travelling from their homes in order to attend.

Some exercises lend themselves to being done out of doors and, in fact, by being taken out of their usual setting, will tend to stimulate the participants to perceive a familiar experience from a completely different perspective. An example of this might be the *Blind walk*. This exercise can be used indoors as a trust exercise in which a person explores his ability to lead and his ability to be dependent upon another person. The exercise can take on the added dimension of providing a sensory and educational experience if it is done out of doors, such as in a wood; particularly if those participating go barefoot. In this instance, a person would become aware of the complexities of the wood using his senses of touch, hearing and smell and thus may perceive aspects of nature that he never noticed before. There are, however, three factors which make it inadvisable to hold a group outside: (1) if the exercise requires considerable concentration, (2) if the group contains some people who are easily distracted, and (3) if the group contains members who are on medication which makes them sensitive to the ultraviolet rays of the sun.

Usually a session and the resulting discussion will be carried out in one location. There are times, however, when this is not advisable and an example of this is when the energy level of the group is very low. If this occurs, a break can be introduced by moving to another room and carrying out the discussion over coffee and cookies. Talking while eating is not only easier, but also tends to unite a group of people and to help them feel more comfortable with one another.

Whatever facilities are available, however, it is important to remember that the suitability of the environment chosen will tend to enhance or detract from the effectiveness of the exercises.

Video-replay techniques

Some of the exercises in this manual are suitable for videotaping and, where we consider this to be so, we have included a footnote to this effect.

Taping a session is done to provide the group with a visual and auditory record of the time they spent together. The tape can also be used as a very effective method of personal evaluation since the replay provides each person with an opportunity to look objectively at his or her own behaviour.

We have used audio-visual replay techniques very successfully with exercises such as the ones in this book. Our experience, however, is that patients are often very anxious when the idea of taping a session is first brought up. We have learned, therefore, to introduce video-replay initially with exercises that are light-hearted (e.g., *theatre games* such as *Action mime, Hand puppets, The matchbox* or *Simultaneous conversations*). The action and replay of these exercises is usually entertaining and does not necessarily have to be analysed. If the video-replay techniques are used with care and sensitivity then they can be extremely rewarding and informative for all the participants.

It is important for the therapist using video-replay to be very familiar with the equipment and its operation. This is because it is impossible to lead a group session calmly and perceptively if one is flustered, and without half the necessary bits and pieces. It is also very important when using video-replay to ascertain from the group members that they are willing to have their group session taped.

THOUGHTS DURING THE SESSION
Presenting the exercise

The method of presentation can, and should be varied, depending on the purpose of the exercise and the needs of the people in the group. For example, a group of professionals in a training session would need a far less simplified explanation than a group of young children or very withdrawn patients.

The therapist should begin by stating clearly the procedure and purpose of the exercise. When giving instructions, it is important to be aware of making them as explicit and concise as possible. The therapist should always enquire before commencing the exercise if everyone has understood the instructions correctly and be prepared to restate specific points if there was anyone who did not follow all of them. This will provide an opportunity for points to be clarified, and give the person who is unassertive a chance to say he does not understand a particular part of the procedure. Once it has been ascertained that everyone has understood the steps in the procedure, the therapist is then in a better position to assess everyone's participation objectively. The job of restating is best done by the co-therapist since he, as a listener, is probably more conscious of any ambiguity.

The leader must know the directions of an exercise well and present them in a positive, assured manner. Many of the exercises may appear silly or childish if the group's confidence is not gained. They should be presented, therefore, in such a way that their usefulness becomes apparent (e.g. as a tool for greater self-awareness and for direct communication). The therapist can also communicate nonverbally with body movements to clarify instructions and invite people to take part in the exercise.

The leader can explain the purpose of an exercise when introducing it by name (e.g. 'Next we are going to do *The chair* which is an exercise to help you feel more comfortable expressing yourself in front of others.'). However, often it is better to move quickly from one exercise to another without any explanation in order to maintain the energy momentum. As the leader you must know the purpose of each exercise, but allow the participants to experience each one spontaneously without any pre-judgement. A discussion can always be held afterwards.

Roles

One important issue which determines the success of a group session is the whole question of leadership and roles.

Initially, leadership is usually assumed by the therapist or teacher. If you are working with another staff member that person becomes your co-therapist. Both the leader and the co-therapist need to be very much involved in a session where exercises are being used. They should:

— participate fully in all parts of an exercise, acting as role models;
— volunteer personal information which is relevant to an exercise, enabling the group members to perceive them as people and to get to know them better;
— be ready to volunteer ideas if the group members are passive;
— volunteer to take their turn spontaneously;
— be aware of everyone in the group and prepared to assist them individually to participate;
— be ready to move onto another exercise at any time if the group members become restless or lose interest;
— avoid being physically next to each other;
— lead the discussion following an exercise or series of exercises; (having given consideration to the focus and how it can be related to the daily lives of the patients) and
— be prepared to hand the leadership over to a group member or members whenever it is appropriate.

Sharing the leadership amongst group members can be achieved by choosing exercises which call for a series of leaders. For example, in *Movement and sound circle* the leader chooses another person to succeed him, in *Word circle* the leadership is taken over by the person who loses the game and in *Mirrors* the leadership is alternated between partners.

During exercises which are primarily verbal, such as *Soapbox debate* and during any of the discussion periods, the leader and co-therapist have these additional duties: to *equalize*, to *focus* and to *link-up*.

To *equalize* is to assist everyone to participate more or less equally. This means that the therapist must first become aware not only of those in the group who tend to monopolise the conversation but also of those who quietly withdraw from it. He must then attempt to bring the quiet people into the conversation, using the topic as a means of entry. The therapist can re-channel the comments of those who are tending to monopolise by repeating or restating what the talkative person has said. Then the therapist can relate it to the topic and direct a question to one of the quieter members, thus inviting him to take part.

To *focus* is to be aware of the topic at all times and to help the group members avoid being sidetracked.

To *link-up* the leader must listen carefully to what is being said and, where necessary, restate what one person has said to another person pointing out where their ideas or experiences are similar. The purpose is to help the participants learn to listen and talk to one another, rather than always directing their comments to you, the therapist.

Sharing of feelings Most people have some difficulty sharing their personal experiences in a group setting. There are, however, various ways in which a therapist can make this easier for everyone concerned. For example, the people participating may feel more relaxed about talking if they are sitting around a small table, or are seated in a small room on some comfortable cushions talking over a cup of coffee.[2]

It is important for the therapist to act as a role-model by being prepared not only to participate in exercises but also to share his own experiences freely. No doubt some people will question the rationale behind this statement maintaining, that a therapist should remain uninvolved if he is to be effective. This is definitely true in some circumstances; however, in our experience this model is not true when utilizing exercises such as these. Remaining uninvolved not only reinforces the thought 'he's the therapist, I'm only the patient,' or 'he's the teacher, I'm only the student,' but it also impedes easy communication. By joining in, the therapist adds credibility to the exercise, enables the people in the group to relate to one another on a more equal basis and encourages more direct and open communication.

From our experience we have found that it is not advisable to force a person to share his feelings or reactions. Everyone has the right to contribute or withhold information and this should be respected. If the situation is not forced initially, a person is far more likely to share his ideas and feelings later on.

The discussion period

The discussion following an exercise is an important time. It is an opportunity to discuss something that has just happened and to begin putting the feelings experienced into words. The problems that a patient encounters during an exercise are often similar to those he experiences during his daily life. The discussion can be used to look more objectively at these difficulties.

The role of the therapist during the discussion is to clarify the purpose of the exercises and to have some questions prepared to stimulate conversation.

Subdividing a group

In some exercises the therapist has the choice of asking people to work in *teams*, in *pairs* or on their own. Division of a group into smaller units must be done with sensitivity and care, and there are many ways of going about it.

Teams. A team is a group of people, who may or may not have a leader, but who have a common purpose. Teams tend to be competitive, and can effect the following responses:

— increased motivation to participate
— increased involvement
— cooperation between members
— a sense of unity within the team because of a common opponent
— enthusiasm and goal directed activity
— a sense of belonging to a smaller defined group

A team is usually smaller in size than the regular group which means that there are fewer people to relate to at any one time. This can be advantageous for the person who has great difficulty becoming involved with others.

Traditionally teams are formed by asking two people to be leaders and to choose their team members from the group. We find this method has very little value when working with people whose self-esteem is low. This is

---

2. Bergel, E. E. (1955). Theory of Commensalism, *Urban Sociology*, p. 181, New York: McGraw-Hill.

because inevitably someone is the last to be chosen. Perhaps the simplest and most efficient method is to number off the participants 'one, two, one, two' and then ask them to form a team with all the other number ones, or number twos respectively. One can also arbitrarily split a group acco to seating arrangement into smaller units. The last way, if you do n to use any of the above methods of team formation, is to leave the i to the group. Suggest they form into two equal teams with an even of men and women on each.

Pairs. A pair is two people who are associated together. The situat a person must work closely with another person during part of an has many positive aspects:

— joint decision-making
— direct interaction with a specific person
— mutual support and ideas
— cooperation
— the sharing of information, experiences and feelings
— caring or taking responsibility for someone specific

For the person who is very uncomfortable relating to a group of people, providing an opportunity in which he can start by relating to just one person is an excellent beginning. Two people constitute the smallest group and this tiny unit can always be enlarged slowly by structuring the situation (e.g. each pair joins another pair to make a foursome, and so on, until the whole group is reformed).

To divide a group into pairs one can invite them to pair up with the person next to them, or give specific instructions such as 'Choose the person who you feel you know best to be your partner'[3] or 'Choose the person who you know least to be your partner'.[4]

Individuals. A person on his own can be very strong or very vulnerable. Many of the people we see in hospitals are often extremely isolated. They have withdrawn from society and exist without much concern for others. An exercise in which a person participates on his own for part of the time is aimed at helping the person see his potentiality as an individual in relation to those around him. Choose exercises carefully so that each person can participate, as best he can, without feeling a failure. Avoid, wherever possible, pointing out a person's weaknesses in front of others since he is probably well aware of them already. Instead concentrate on assisting him to acknowledge his strengths. Working on one's own can offer the following opportunities:

— to see one's ideas put into effect
— to make decisions
— to take on responsibility
— to share and care for others
— to lead

---

3. Appropriate to use for the exercise *Blind walk*, p. 40.
4. Appropriate to use for the exercise *Introductions*, p. 118.

— to look objectively at oneself, both strengths and weaknesses
— to improve skills
— to experience success
— to become more self-confident
— to realize the effect of one's actions upon others

In summary then, whether you choose to have the group members work alone, in pairs or in teams, make this decision on the basis of their needs and abilities.

AFTERTHOUGHTS
Post group evaluation

Once a group session is over and the discussion period with the group has come to an end, it is advisable to get together with the co-therapist and other staff members. This ten minute post group meeting is the most advantageous time to both assess the group and to plan for the following session. During it each group member, the group as a whole, the exercises used and any drawings or written material resulting should be given consideration.

Assessment of individuals

Throughout the exercises in the book we have listed, opposite the steps in the procedure, the usefulness of these steps in observing certain aspects of a person's behaviour. From these observations assessments can be made and some conclusions drawn about each person's progress.

The following is a list of some of the observations that can be made:

Appearance and behaviour
Form of talk
Orientation
Mood
Thought content
Distortions of thought content
Obsessive-compulsive behaviours
Sensorial faculties
 (i) Memory
 (ii) Concentration
 (iii) Comprehension
Intelligence
Insight
Ability to express feelings
Interpersonal skills
Response to authority
Leadership ability
Spontaneity
Coordination

Evaluation of the group

The group as a whole must also be evaluated. Consider first the predominant feeling in the group (e.g. *anger*). If many of the members were angry, did you recognize it in time to use exercises that allowed the members to express or accept their anger? Did you initiate a discussion to help them investigate the cause of this anger? If the cause was known but the solution not attainable, did you use gross physical movement to allow an acceptable display of this anger? If you should have a similar mood in a future group, what would you change in order to handle it better?

Then consider the participation of the group members. Did they take part or was there a sense of reluctance? Did they interact with one another or maintain their isolation? Was the energy generated by the group high or low? Did the group members lead the discussion or did you, as the therapist, have to initiate all the questions and comments? As a result of the work done during the session do you have a clear *focus* for the next group?

Choice of exercises

This is the time to refer back to the *focus* of the group session and think about whether the exercises chosen were appropriate or not. Ask yourself if the session met your expectations as well as the needs of the patients. If it did not, ask yourself why. Was it that you chose inappropriate exercises or perhaps the appropriate ones, but in an awkward sequence? Did you spend enough time *warming up*? Were the exercises active enough to involve all members? Were they too active thereby excluding some people? Were they too intellectual? Was the content too abstract for the majority of the group members? Had the group evolved to a stage that allowed the members to share the feeling material you were seeking?

Think also about whether you were sufficiently well prepared and if the location you chose was a good one. Were the exercises selected suitable for the number of people in the group and, finally, did you present the exercises in the most understandable way? If you can answer these questions you will learn from both your mistakes and your successes.

Projective technique material

It is wise to identify any projective technique material produced in the group, with the date, name of exercise and any comments. This should be done following the group and saved for your records and perhaps for research use later. Material that the group members have produced can be displayed but only after you have obtained the individual group member's permission to do so. These drawings or diagrams express, diagramatically, some very sensitive areas in the member's lives and any wishes to keep this material private must be treated with respect.

Displayed drawings can often be used as a shorthand reference for yourself and the group members if the same subject matter occurs in a subsequent group. The picture will help quick recall of the information the group members conveyed. Group productions can also be displayed. This material gives each person a sense of belonging as it shows a joint effort, composed of contributions, representing the personalities of the members involved.

Chronological record

For your own reference you may wish to record the progress of each group. To be brief and concise, we suggest recording:
  (1) the date
  (2) the number of people who attended
  (3) the number of staff
  (4) the major goal or focus of the group
  (5) the mood of the group
  (6) the exercises used to obtain that goal

(7) a good to bad rating scale of the success of each exercise with explanatory comments

Charting   Often very significant material comes out of a group, especially from those members who become less inhibited when doing nonverbal techniques. This material should be recorded as soon as possible on the member's chart or file. Photographs of significant projective technique material can also be included if the budget permits.

The last thing to think about in the process of evaluation is the next session. As we have mentioned before, each successive group should build on the momentum and experience of the previous one. When planning the next group, therefore, one should consider if any situation arose during the last group which could be used as a springboard. Often the group members are just beginning to share their ideas and feelings freely as it is time to end the session. If through an exercise at the beginning of the next session you are able to reconstruct the same level of communication at an earlier stage in the group process you will watch your group grow quickly and the goals you had set out for it attained.

AWARENESS OF OTHERS

Find the change

This is an exercise to increase the individual's ability to perceive another person accurately and to be innovative.

Recommended for these problems
— *social isolation*
— *egocentricity*
— *distorted body image*
— *poor concentration*

Stage of group development
This exercise could be used as an introductory exercise, or if the individuals in the group know each other well, as a *warm-up* exercise.

Synopsis
It takes the form of a game where two teams line up so that each player stands opposite a player from the other team. One team then turns to face the wall while each person in the other team changes three things about his appearance. On turning around, the first team must try to spot the changes. When each team has completed this, the number of changes can be increased.

Materials and equipment
Materials to keep the score.

Procedure

Invite the participants to form two teams of equal numbers[1]	To offer the experience of working together with a small number of people towards a common goal
Explain the exercise as follows: 'Would each team please form a line so that every player is paired off with and standing opposite a player from the other team. Stand about one metre apart'	To ensure that each person is standing in front of and reasonably close to another person and, thereby, assisting them to be aware of one another
Identify the teams (e.g., *A* and *B*)	To give each team a separate identity which encourages team spirit

---

1. Description of the formation of teams in the chapter *Some basic concepts*.

Ask if there is a volunteer to do the scoring. (If the number of participants is even, the therapist will need to take the volunteer's place in his team)	This provides an opportunity for someone who feels very unsure, or that the exercise is beneath him, to take a nonchallenging leadership role. Scoring introduces a competitive element to the exercise. Competition gives a sense of purpose and tends to encourage a person to try harder.
'Will each person on Team *A* take a good long look at your partner's appearance	To encourage each person to look closely at another person
'When you think you have noticed all the details, turn your back on your partner	This involves making a decision
'Team *B*, when everyone in Team *A* has their backs to you, each of you will change three things about your appearance[2]	To encourage awareness of the other team and provide an opportunity to be innovative and subtle
'Let Team *A* know when you are ready	To encourage cooperation
'On turning around, Team *A*, try and spot the three changes your partner has made'	To encourage verbal interaction and provide an opportunity for receiving immediate comments with regard to the accuracy of one's observations
Invite the scorer to record the total number of correct observations	To give this person an opportunity to interact with some or all of the group members
Repeat the exercise for Team *B*	

Comments

---

2. For example, undo a button that was done up, turn up your collar, change rings on fingers, and so on.

Nicknames

This is a *warm-up* exercise. It stimulates group members to be physically active and helps them get to know each other better.

Recommended for these problems
— *social isolation*
— *difficulty talking to new acquaintances*
— *psychomotor retardation*

Stage of group development
This is an excellent exercise to use with a group of people who do not know one another.

Synopsis
Each person identifies himself on a name tag. The object of the game is to be the first person to record on paper everyone else's name.

Materials and equipment
A spacious room
Pencils
Name tags
Pins
Sheets of paper.

Procedure

Explain the exercise as follows:
'Write on your name tag your nickname or a name
that describes you

'Pin the tag to the back of your sleeve
'When I say "start," move around, read and write
down all the names you can see

With the name tag in this position the person has to move about in order to avoid being identified. This encourages (1) an increased awareness of his position in relation to those around him and (2) defensive tactics as he attempts to trick others into revealing their identity

---

'The first person to collect all the names (the number
in the group) is the winner'

Discussion topics   — When three or more people have completed their lists, then sit down together and ask each person to identify himself.
— Encourage discussion about how each person acquired his nickname. This will help satisfy the curiosity of those who had not finished and give an opportunity for jovial feedback between individuals.

Comments

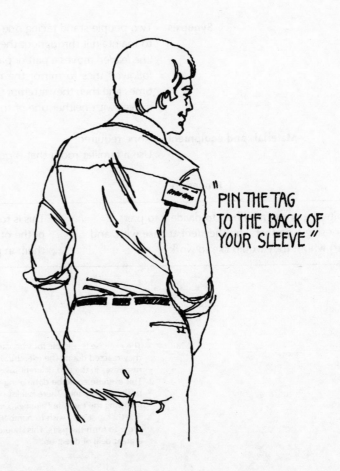

"PIN THE TAG
TO THE BACK OF
YOUR SLEEVE"

Allow 5–15 minutes # Mirrors

This is an exercise to help a person improve his ability to communicate and interact with another person.[1]

Recommended for these problems
— *social isolation*
— *poor eye-contact*
— *distorted body image*
— *poor concentration*
— *inhibited self-expression*

Stage of group development
This is an appropriate exercise to use when there is little interaction between group members.

Synopsis
Two people stand facing one another. First they make eye-contact and try to maintain it throughout the remainder of the exercise. Then, one of them (*the leader*) moves a part or parts of his body very slowly and his partner (*the follower*) tries to mirror the motion exactly. The pair switch roles several times and then they attempt to continue moving and reflecting each other's moves with neither one of them consciously leading.

Materials and equipment
None required[2]
Use a familiar room that is quiet.

Procedure

Invite the group members to divide into pairs,[3] choosing a partner who they feel at ease with, and with whom they would like to work	This is to encourage each person to become aware of the other group members and to contact one of them in particular

1. The exercise is suitable for *videotaping*. The replay will enable the participants to see how they reacted during the exercise. They will be able to view their emotional and physical responses in the two different roles.
2. This exercise could be done using music as a means of suggesting patterns of movement to the participants. There is a list of pieces of music that could be used, immediately following the exercise *Painting to music*, p. 106.
3. The therapist may wish to number off the group members, one, two, one, two, etc., in order to form the pairs. This should not really be necessary unless the group requires a great deal of direction.

Explain the exercise as follows:
'Stand about one metre away from your partner and look him firmly in the eye

For those people who find making and maintaining eye-contact very difficult it is important that they have a chance to practise. If everyone does the exercise simultaneously it will help those who are at all self-conscious

'When you both feel comfortable, decide between you who will be the *leader* and who will be the *follower*

This requires cooperation and decision-making between the two people

'Then, looking each other in the eye as continuously as possible, . . .

Maintaining eye-contact requires considerable concentration

'I would like the *leader* to start moving his body or a part of it *very, very* slowly. (Stress the last part)

This provides an opportunity for a person to lead and initiate actions, in a controlled and deliberate way

'At the same time as you do this your partner will try to mirror your action exactly'

This requires concentration and will exercise the *follower's* ability to perceive and mime body movements initiated by his partner

Allow each pair to practise, giving assistance or demonstration where it is necessary

To encourage everyone to become involved in the doing of the exercise and to assist them in carrying out the instructions correctly

Then invite the pairs to switch roles, so that the former *leader* becomes the *follower* and vice versa	This enables everyone to experience both roles, and may encourage versatility
When each pair has switched roles several times, continue by giving the following instructions:	
'Now I would like you to move in free form: that is, with neither one of you consciously leading or following and yet each of you continuing to mirror the movements of the other'	This encourages sensitivity to another person and the experience of working simultaneously with him; it also requires greater concentration
When the exercise is over, ask the group members to sit in a circle	
Invite them to discuss any feelings or reactions they may have experienced	To encourage the sharing of feelings evoked by an experience common to all and particularly related to the difference between being the *leader* and the *follower*

Discussion topics
— How did it feel to make eye-contact with another person?
— Was it easy or difficult to maintain eye-contact?
— Discuss the importance of looking at people in order to communicate more effectively.
— Discuss any differences you experienced in *leading* or *following*.

Comments

Facial expressions

This is an exercise which illustrates the part facial expression plays in communication between people.[1]

Recommended for these problems
— *poor self-awareness*
— *difficulty talking in a group situation*
— *low self-esteem*
— *flat affect*[2]
— *poor concentration*[3]

Stage of group development
This is an excellent exercise for a group of withdrawn, depressed people. The group members need not know one another very well but some familiarity may be helpful if they are to work together easily.

Synopsis
The group members make a collage of faces, each one of which has been selected to show a different expression. The members then discuss each face and attempt to identify the underlying feeling or feelings. Finally, using the collage as a resource if necessary, each person mimes one of the previously identified feelings for the group to guess.

Materials and equipment[4]
A wide variety of magazines
Scissors
Glue
A large sheet of paper e.g., 60 cm × 90 cm (on a separate table)
Felt pens
Small slips of paper and a container
Room which is large enough to provide adequate working space.

---

1. The second and third parts of this exercise are suitable for *videotaping*. When the replay is watched players will be able to see their own attempts at using their faces to express feelings. The replay will also bring into focus the fact that besides facial expression, feelings can be effectively communicated using body posture, body movements and gestures.
2. This exercise is particularly useful for patients whose faces tend to be expressionless and who are unaware of this fact. It can also be a rewarding experience for those who believe that no one can guess how they are feeling at a particular point in time.
3. The fact that the exercise is composed of three distinct parts means that it tends to re-focus the attention of patients who have difficulty maintaining contact with reality for long periods of time.
4. To promote a sense of responsibility, involve several or all of the group members in the collection and return of the materials used and in the preparation of the room.

Procedure

Invite the group members to gather around the table	To encourage a sense of group cohesiveness
Give the following instructions: 'From the magazines provided, select and cut out a number of faces of people'	To promote active individual participation and exercise the capacities of choice and motor coordination
(Sometimes it is useful to limit the number of faces to be selected by each person, e.g., two to five)	This gives the participants limits within which to work and may help to reduce any anxiety arising through the tendency to be overinclusive. If the group is large and the attention span of the members short, this will also ensure that the collage contains a reasonable amount of resource material and yet represents each person
'Try to choose a variety of expressions'	To encourage discrimination through paying attention to detail as well as to assist recall of the wide range of emotions
'When you have made your selection, paste these faces on the large sheet of paper to form a collage'[5]	To encourage goal directed behaviour and cooperative interaction with the other participants
When this part of the exercise has been completed explain the next part: 'We now need two volunteers, a *leader* and a *secretary*.	To provide an opportunity for transferring leadership from the therapist to the group members
'The *leader* will select one of the faces on the collage and point to it. He will invite the rest of us to decide what feeling or feelings we consider the face is expressing	This requires decisions by both the *leader* and participants, together with mutual cooperation. It provides a check for the accuracy of individual perceptions. It may also help to increase descriptive vocabulary and stimulate awareness of the range of feelings
'When the majority of us agree, the *secretary* will record this feeling on a slip of paper, which he will fold and place in a container'	To help the *leader* exercise his diplomacy and ability to recognize a final or majority decision
Inviting the group to gather around the collage, proceed with the exercise until all or most of the faces have been discussed	

5. You can choose one or two people to paste the faces on to the paper. It is best if this job is given either to a person who feels cutting out pictures is beneath him or to a person who is restless. It provides an opportunity for leadership and making decisions.

Then remove the collage and ask the group to sit in a circle	This physical activity tends to promote renewed interest
In turn, invite each person to pick one of the slips of paper out of the container and mime the feeling written on it, for the group to guess[6]	To provide an opportunity for each person to experiment with the use of a larger range of facial expressions for which he receives recognition and feedback
At the end, ask the group members if they have any comments on the exercise	To encourage the participants to discuss the importance of observing and understanding facial expression as an aid to successful communication

Discussion topics
— The ease or difficulty with which the participants were able to mime emotions.
— How any particular facial expression may affect others and thus our relationships.
— In what other ways do we express feelings nonverbally?

Comments[7]

---

6. Keep the collage as a visual stimulus for those people who are unable to remember or mime a particular facial expression.
7. Ask the group members individually, in pairs, or in groups, to find pictures of faces to illustrate some or all of the following feelings:
Boredom, trust, repulsion, relief, loneliness, hate, joy, anger, fear, contentment, strength, unfulfilment, support, confusion, shyness, inferiority, involvement, frustration, superiority, suspicion, attraction, hurt, love, sadness, affection, hope, weakness, satisfaction, rejection, or curiosity.
This would be valuable for patients who need more structure and/or whose descriptive abilities are severely impaired. It is a suggested variation.
Discussion could be based on comparing and contrasting the pictures each group found to illustrate similar feelings or on the appropriateness of the pictures selected.

Masks

This is an exercise in self-awareness which focuses on how people use their facial expression as a means of defence.

Recommended for these problems
— *lack of insight*
— *withdrawal*
— *difficulty expressing feelings*

Stage of group development
This exercise is suitable to use with a group that has worked together for a few sessions and whose members are beginning to trust one another.

Synopsis
Each person is asked to draw his own face twice, firstly in terms of how others see it, and secondly in terms of how he actually feels inside. The group then discuss the resulting pictures.

Materials and equipment
Sheets of moderately stiff paper, about 20 cm × 28 cm
Felt pens (wide colour range)
Pencils
Room with a table and chairs.

Procedure

Invite the group members to sit around the table . . .	To promote a sense of group cohesion and a purposeful atmosphere
and each to take two sheets of paper	This encourages each person to make the decision whether he will participate in the exercise or not
Place the felt pens in the centre of the table	To encourage cooperative interaction while working
Give the following instructions: 'On one of your pieces of paper draw a picture of your face which shows how you think it appears to other people. Title this *How I appear to others*	To assist each person to be objective with regard to his outward appearance
When everyone has finished, continue with the second part of the exercise	

'Now, thinking carefully of how you feel inside, draw another picture of your face (using the second piece of paper) to show how you actually feel. Title this *How I actually feel'*

To increase the awareness of feelings at a particular point in time and to assist differentiation between outward and inward expression of them
To aid the therapist's assessment of each person's mental state

---

When everyone has finished both parts of the exercise, invite each person to show the group his two drawings and to explain them

To provide each person with an opportunity to explain his own drawings and promote increased awareness amongst everyone of how facial expression can be used to mask real feelings

---

Encourage the group members to discuss any ideas or reactions they may have

---

Also invite them to become more aware of how often they notice themselves and others using their *mask* rather than expressing their real feelings

This may promote greater self-awareness and encourage the giving and receiving of personal comments

---

Note: Displaying the *masks* on the walls of the group's room can act as a reminder to them of the exercise

---

Discussion topics — What are the reasons for masking one's feelings?
— What are the effects upon oneself and others of masking one's feelings?
— How does each person's self-image compare with how other people see him?

Comments

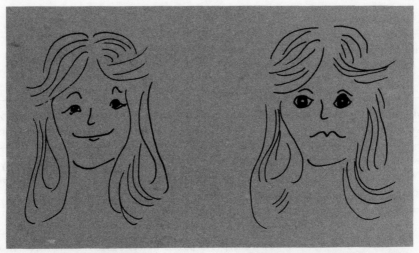

HOW I APPEAR   HOW I ACTUALLY FEEL

Theme collage

This is an exercise to promote group cohesion through the nonverbal and verbal interaction which occurs when a group of people work together.

Recommended for these problems
— *difficulty with social interaction*
— *withdrawal*
— *anxiety*
— *poverty of ideas*

Stage of group development
This is a valuable exercise to use with a group that lacks cohesion and contains a number of very isolated members.

Synopsis
The group choose a theme together and then compose a collage which represents each person's perception of that theme. The collage is then displayed.

Materials and equipment
Magazines
Scissors
Glue and glue pots
Felt pens
Large sheet of paper
Newspaper
Use a large working table and chairs around it.

Procedure

Explain the exercise as follows: 'We are going to make a collage using magazine pictures	
'First, however, we have to choose a theme.[1] Does anyone have any suggestions?	This part of the exercise requires a group decision which is the first step toward cohesion
'Then I would like you to go through the magazines and find pictures or examples of that theme. Cut the pictures out'	This gives each person an opportunity for self-expression and personal interpretation of the theme

1. Give a few examples for possible themes, e.g., Leisure-time, Anger, Family life, Things I have enjoyed.

Ask the first group member who appears restless to arrange the contributions for the collage on a sheet of background paper. Engage the next restless person to assist him in sticking them on[2]

Giving this job to the person who finds the first part of the exercise difficult, perhaps due to anxiety or poor concentration, will provide him with a constructive outlet for his restlessness

Make sure each group member is represented by at least one contribution

This ensures that the collage is a group product and represents each person's involvement in the task (e.g., his feelings, his past experiences, his ideas as they relate to the theme, etc.)

'When the collage is complete we will discuss the theme and the pictures that each of us chose'

To promote discussion amongst the participants

Suggest that the group hang the collage up

Once hung the collage is a visual display of the group's ability to work together

Discussion topics
— How easy or difficult was it to find pictures that related to the theme?
— Why did each person choose his particular pictures?
— What were your feelings about the theme?
— How did the group work together and what part did each person play in the task?

Comments

---

2. Arranging and pasting the pictures could also be a group task requiring cooperation, compromise, decision-making and imagination on everyone's part.

If she were a flower . . . ?

This is an exercise which promotes group cohesion: at the same time it is an enjoyable means through which both self-knowledge and awareness of others can be obtained.[1] [2]

Recommended for these problems[3]
— low self-confidence
— poor self-awareness
— social isolation

Stage of group development
This exercise takes the form of a *theatre game*. Each group member takes a turn at guessing the identity of a fellow group member from clues given him about that member's personality.

Materials and equipment
A comfortable, quiet space.

Procedure

Sit comfortably in a circle

Explain the exercise as follows:
'I am going to leave the room and while I am gone I would like you to choose someone to be the mystery person. When I return I will try to guess that person's identity by asking questions about his or her personality. However, I must pretend that this person could become any object (rather than a human being) and all my questions will be asking what type of object would that person be. For example, I will ask "If she were an animal, which animal would she be?" When thinking of your answer consider what the person chosen is like and then choose an animal that has similar characteristics'

To show how the game is played by personal demonstration. This will clarify the verbal instructions

---

1. See Suggestions at the end of the exercise for alternatives to the category *Flower*.
2. The exercise is suitable for *videotaping*. The tape will provide an accurate record of the feedback that a person received and bring to his attention points that he may have missed during the exercise. Often people have difficulty accepting compliments and only remember the criticisms.
3. Contraindicated for those schizophrenic patients who become more confused when they are asked to use abstract thinking.

Ask each member to describe the mystery person in terms of the category chosen. 'If you can identify the person from their answers, name him; if not choose another category'

In this process three things happen:
(1) The mystery person is able to hear the other group members' impressions of him (2) each group member has to think deeply about the personality characteristics of another group member and (3) the therapist is able to assess how each individual views other people

Once the identity of the mystery person has been guessed, that person becomes the next player and leaves the room and a new mystery person is chosen

Discussion topics
— What personal qualities are the most obvious?
— What qualities did the members see in the mystery person and how did they describe them?

Suggestions for
'If she were a flower'

What type of flower?	What kind of music?
What make of car?	What sort of house?
What colour?	What sort of dance steps?
What household appliance?	What kind of body of water?
What animal?	What type of transportation?
What piece of clothing?	What type of boat?
What kind of chair?	What vegetable?
	What kind of tool?

Comments

Murder

This is an exercise in nonverbal communication. It requires an awareness of other people and the ability to make eye-contact.[1]

Recommended for these problems
— *poor eye-contact*
— *poor concentration*
— *social isolation*
— *egocentricity*

Stage of group development   Since this is a relatively non-threatening exercise[2] it can be used with a group of people who do not interact with one another readily.

Synopsis   The exercise takes the form of a puzzle game where one player as the *Murderer* murders the other players by catching their eye and winking at them. The object of the game is to identify the *Murderer* before being murdered oneself.

Materials and equipment   Playing cards
Select one playing card for each person playing the game; include a *Joker* in the selection
The game can be played anywhere.

Procedure

Invite everyone[3] to sit in a circle	This encourages a sense of group cohesiveness and also ensures that everyone can see each other easily
Explain the exercise as follows: The cards have been shuffled and one will be dealt to each person[4]	The person who is dealer is placed in the position of making direct contact with every other player
'When you receive your card, look at it, but do not reveal what it is to anyone else	This introduces a puzzle element to the game and should stimulate more interest and attention

1. This exercise is contraindicated for anyone who is very suspicious, or who feels that a person, or people in general, wish to harm him.
2. It is an excellent technique for children or for adults who need a fun *warm-up* exercise.
3. The game can be played with any number of people. It is more difficult with a larger number though and requires greater concentration and attention.
4. The group leader can demonstrate how to be *dealer* but should hand this responsibility over to a group member as soon as possible.

'If you have been dealt the *Joker* you are the *Murderer*. Do not let anyone know this

The *Murderer* can murder another player by catching his eye and winking at him	This requires being constantly aware of everyone, making eye-contact and communicating a message without speaking
'Once you have been winked at, or rather *murdered*, wait a short while and then say "I'm dead". You may remain seated but are now out of the game	At this point an individual must take the initiative to relay information to the rest of the group
The object of the game is for those who are still *alive* to identify the *Murderer*. The *Murderer* however will try to murder everyone before being caught	To do this the players have to constantly scan the eyes of all the other players
'Once you think you know who the *Murderer* is, name the person. If you are correct the game is over and if you are wrong you forfeit your *life*'	This is an opportunity for an individual to make a decision and act on it

Discussion topics
— What did you have to do in order to identify the *Murderer*?
— If you were the *Murderer* how did you try to avoid being caught or noticed?
— Discuss the advantages of being aware of people around you.

Comments

AWARENESS OF SELF

Life positions

This is a *warm-up* exercise designed to stimulate the participants by physical activity and to provide an opportunity for them to be aggressive in a non-verbal and constructive way. In the exercise the participants can also explore their role in life as related to the submissive/dominant continuum.[1]

Recommended for these problems
— *lack of assertiveness*
— *difficulty expressing feelings*
— *anxiety*

Stage of group development
The exercise is appropriate for a group whose members need a constructive outlet for their energy.[2]

Synopsis
The group members are divided into small teams. In each team the leader is denoted as being the most dominant and the last person as the least dominant. The team members then fight, without speaking, for the position on their team in which they feel most comfortable.

Materials and equipment
None
Use a room which is carpeted and has a long vacant wall with plenty of free space in front of it.

Procedure

Randomly select three people[3] (e.g., A, B and C) and ask them to stand facing the wall and about two to three metres apart

Then ask the remaining group members (See 'X' in the diagram) to line up behind A, B and C to form teams of approximately equal numbers

In this way each person is given the opportunity to make an initial decision, (namely, which team he/she would like to be in), and to follow through on it

```
          A    X X X X X
WALL      B    X X X X X
          C    X X X X X
```

1. The exercise has proven to be very stimulating and an excellent means of increasing group cohesion and verbal participation.
2. Caution should be exercised if some group members are in poor physical condition.
3. The number chosen will depend on the number of people in the group, as each team should have at least five members.

Explain the exercise as follows:
'The position closest to the wall will be held by the most dominant person in your team. The position at the back of the team will be held by the least dominant person. Those positions in between represent degrees of dominance between the two extremes

'Bearing this in mind and without speaking, I would like you to fight physically for the position on your team in which you personally feel most comfortable'

To encourage physical contact and expression of feelings in a nonverbal manner

Allow the teams to fight on until each person is satisfied with the position he/she attains[4]

Then invite each team to sit down where they are[5] and discuss amongst themselves their reactions to the exercise before sharing them with the whole group

Discussion topics
— How does the physical contact affect you? Discuss:
  (a) fears
  (b) associated feelings – positive or negative, and
  (c) how each person fought
— What reaction does each person have to the others and the positions they finally chose?
— What reasons did each person have for choosing his final position?
— How does each person's behaviour during the game relate to his daily life? Is this how he deals with friends, family situations, work, etc.? Is it appropriate and satisfactory? Is it how he likes to be? Does he achieve his goals?

Comments

4. Coaching by therapist – 'no sharing of positions.'
   – 'no speaking.'
5. If the number of teams is large and the therapist wishes to demonstrate the technique (e.g., to other professionals) then it is practical that one team only discusses while everyone else observes.

Allow 20–30 minutes # Blind walk

This is an exercise to increase trust and sensory awareness.[1]

Recommended for these problems
— *apathy*
— *social isolation*
— *difficulty trusting people*

Stage of group development
This exercise is appropriate to use with a group whose members are acquainted but are having difficulty trusting one another.

Synopsis
The exercise requires that the group members form pairs and take it in turns to be led about a room, with their eyes closed. During this blind walk the person has to try to identify objects to which he has been guided (or people to whom his partner has introduced him).

Materials and equipment
None
Use a familiar room which has furniture in it.[2]

Procedure

Invite the group members to choose a partner with whom they feel comfortable	To initiate social interaction and decision-making
Explain the exercise as follows: 'Will each pair decide between them who is to be the *leader* and who is to be the *blindman*	To encourage cooperative interaction and provide an opportunity for choosing either a dominant or a submissive role in relation to the other person
'Will the *blindman* close his eyes and try to keep them closed throughout the exercise	This will provide him with the experience of placing himself in the care of another person
'Meanwhile, the *leader* will gently guide his partner around the room making sure that he does not hurt himself	To encourage a sense of responsibility and protectiveness towards another person To give some degree of physical contact

1. The exercise is suitable for *videotaping*. The replay can be used to show the relationships between partners. The tape will also record the subtle nonverbal reactions of participants which can be used as a basis for discussion.
2. Go outdoors to provide a different experience.

'When you feel the *blindman* trusts you . . .

To help develop awareness of how his partner is feeling as expressed by body movements

'take his hand and guide it toward objects[3] in the room, inviting him to identify them through his sense of touch

To increase the capacity for accurately perceiving things using senses other than sight, and to provide an opportunity for enjoying the world in this way

'Do this for five[4] minutes and then change roles so that the *leader* becomes the *blindman* and vice versa'

When this part of the exercise is over, invite the group members to sit in a circle[5] and share their feelings about the experience

"INVITING HIM TO IDENTIFY OBJECTS THROUGH HIS SENSE OF TOUCH"

3. When the group has experienced and is at ease identifying objects, the exercise can be extended so that each *blindman* is required to identify other group members by touch. The purpose of this variation is to help overcome the fear of touching other people and to promote the idea that this can be a pleasant and rewarding experience.
4. The time limit is arbitrary, but should be long enough to enable the *blindman* to become relaxed and at ease, and short enough to prevent him becoming bored.
5. To improve confidence by providing the opportunity for sharing feelings firstly with one other person and then with a gradually increasing number, invite each person to sit opposite his partner. Ask the two of them to share their feelings and reactions towards the exercise with each other and then to invite another pair to join them so that the four of them share their experiences. Continue in this manner until the whole group is involved in one discussion.

Discussion topics — What was the difference between the dominant (leader) and submissive (blindman) roles?

— What was it like to touch objects and people? What feelings did this arouse?

— Were you able to place your trust in another person?

— Were you afraid of bumping into objects and hurting yourself?

— How did you react?

— Did you experience any sensations from the environment?

— What were you aware of?

— Did you sense how your partner was feeling? How?

— What characteristics did you remember about the people you were introduced to?

— Why is it important to notice things about people?

— How does being observant help one's relationships?

Comments

Where am I?

...reness of oneself and others in terms of
...uum and (2) the ability to express

Recommended for t...

Stage of...

...pressing feelings

...imulate a discussion[1] and is appropriate for
...me sense of group identity. It is a valuable
...oup energy is low.

...n an imaginary line to show firstly, how he sees
...group and, secondly, how he would like to
...then encouraged by giving each person an
...position or positions that he took.

...ne white and one coloured
...e to allow everyone to stand in a line.

Invite ...
This physical movement encourages an attitude of
readiness for the exercise

Explain the exercise as ...
'I am going to call this corner of the ro... ...
leader and the opposite corner *withdrawn, follower*...
so that these represent the extremes of possible
participation in the group'

---

1. This exercise may be appropriate to use when participation by the majority of group members is generally passive perhaps with the exception of one or two members who take very active roles.
Through this technique, the quieter members are presented with an opportunity to say how they would like to participate and what is hindering them. The active ones are given a chance to explain why they are more involved.

Enquire if everyone understands	This allows anyone who was not listening to ask for the instructions to be repeated or re-phrased
'Imagine that there ia a line drawn between these two corners	
'Think about how you, personally, participate in the group and then . . .	To encourage self-awareness and . . .
'place yourself somewhere on the imaginary line to show this	provide a chance for each person to express his conclusion nonverbally
'You will find that the position you choose is relative to those that the other people in the group choose	To develop an increased awareness of others
'Mark your position by writing your name, using the white chalk[2]	This will act as a visual aid in the discussion part of the exercise
'Now ask yourself if this is where you would most like to be and . . .	To encourage the individual to consider his ideal behaviour in contrast to his actual behaviour and express the former in a nonverbal way
'if it is not, then take a second position on the imaginary line, to show how you would prefer to participate	
'If you are content with your present participation in the group then stay where you are	This is to encourage each person to be honest
'Mark your position even if you have not moved using the coloured chalk'	
When everyone has done this, invite the group members to sit in a circle around the marked positions	To bring the group members into a position that is not only more conducive to discussion but also enables them to observe the positions that everyone else took
Invite each person to talk about the reasons he had for taking his particular position, or positions, along the imaginary line . . .	To encourage each person to express his ideas and feelings in a direct way
and encourage the group to discuss these	By understanding each other's behaviour the group members are likely to become more supportive of one another

2. Wait until everyone has chosen and marked their position before proceeding with the next part of the exercise.

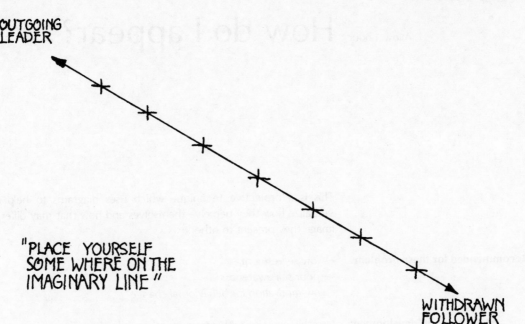

OUTGOING
LEADER

"PLACE YOURSELF
SOME WHERE ON THE
IMAGINARY LINE"

WITHDRAWN
FOLLOWER

Discussion topics   — How does the position each person chose relate to their participation in the group?
— Does each person's participation in the group have any relationship to his lifestyle, work, friendships, and methods of coping with problems?

Comments

How do I appear?

This is a projective technique which uses diagrams to help members verbalize how they perceive themselves and how that may differ from the image they present to others.

Recommended for these problems
— *low self-esteem*
— *poor self-awareness*
—*low motivation for behavioural change*

Stage of group development
Use this exercise with group members who have formed some bonds of trust and are willing to share feelings with each other.

Synopsis
Three drawings are made by each person to contrast outward appearances with personal identity and to help suggest ways of changing.

Materials and equipment
Table and chairs
Pencils with erasers
White paper.

Procedure

Hand out a sheet of paper and pencil to each person

Ask them to fold their sheet of paper into thirds. Demonstrate with your own paper

At this point the therapist can assess which members have difficulty following directions

---

Explain the exercise as follows:
'Label the first third of your paper *How others see me,* the middle third *How I see myself,* and the final third *How I would like to be seen*

'Now draw diagrams and symbols to depict yourself in each of the three areas'

Using symbols rather than words may release feelings from below the conscious and, therefore, censorable level

---

When most people seem to have finished ask 'Does anyone need more time?'

To give those who are not ready the responsibility for informing the group when they are finished

When everyone has completed the exercise, ask each person to explain his set of diagrams to the group. Encourage the group members to respond honestly when each person is discussing the category *How others see me*. Be prepared to help each person handle confrontation. Encourage the group members to be constructive with any critical feedback they may give

This gives each person an opportunity to see if his perceptions about how others view him are correct

---

Discussion topics   — Being misunderstood
— Appearances are deceiving
— Putting forward a favourable image
— Accuracy of self-perception.

Comments

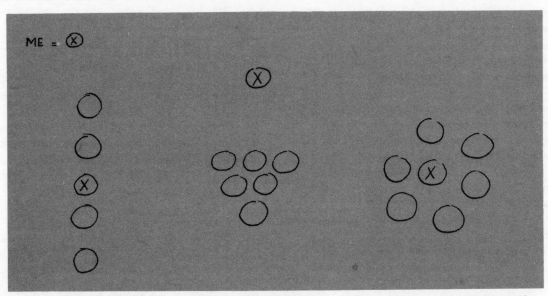

HOW OTHERS SEE ME   HOW I SEE MYSELF   HOW I WOULD LIKE TO BE SEEN

Now and the future

This is an exercise which assists individuals to gain a deeper understanding of themselves and of each other.

Recommended for these problems
— *lack of insight*
— *difficulty making decisions*
— *low motivation for behavioural change*

Stage of group development
This exercise is best for a group that has developed some unity and in which the members have some interest in each other.

Synopsis
Each person compares his present situation with his desired future situation, depicting both of them in diagramatic form.

Materials and equipment
White paper
Pencils and Erasers
Felt pens
Table and chairs.

Procedure

Invite everyone to sit around the table and help themselves to paper and pencils

---

Ask the group members to fold their paper in half (demonstrate with your own paper)

Give the following instructions:
'On the left side of your piece of paper draw *how you are now*. That is, how you are feeling and what your present life situation is. Then on the right side draw *how you wish to be in the future*. Draw diagrams and symbols to explain your situation, *don't* be artistic or draw a self-portrait'

To give the individual an opportunity to look at his present situation clearly and to project himself into a future relieved of his present problems

---

When most people are finished ask
'Does anyone need more time?'

To allow those people who either have much to say or who find the exercise difficult, to work at their own speed. They will take the responsibility for telling the group when they are ready

---

When the group is ready, ask who would like to begin by explaining his drawings. If the discussion is awkward ask him to compare the two drawings and explain how he hopes to attain his desired future

To stimulate some dynamic thoughts about life as he sees it and possible changes he can make

Discussion topics
— Discuss methods of changing present situations.
— Discuss fear of the future (e.g., jobs and other commitments).
— What it is like to feel helpless about making decisions for your life.
— Discuss taking on responsibility for one's own life and it's direction.

Comments

HOW I AM NOW   HOW I WISH TO BE IN THE FUTURE

Allow 1 hour or more

Who am I?

This is an exercise in self-awareness and self-expression.

Recommended for these problems
— *social isolation*
— *identity crisis*
— *poor self-concept*
— *difficulty expressing feelings*[1]

Stage of group development This exercise is very appropriate to use with a group containing many new members.

Synopsis The technique takes the form of a self portrait collage which each person makes to illustrate his personality and *life space*.[2] It is followed by an opportunity for him to explain and discuss his portrayed identity with the other group members.

Materials and equipment Sheets of paper approximately 60 cm × 90 cm, one for each person[3]
Wide selection of magazines
Scissors
Glue
Overalls (Optional)
Use a room which has sufficient working space or tables for the number of participants.[4]

Procedure

Explain the exercise as follows:
'We are going to make individual collages. Imagine that a friend wishes to know all about you, but you are unable to speak

A clear explanation is needed to allay fears of having to perform and perhaps be judged

---

1. This is an excellent technique to use with patients who have recently arrived in hospital or any other treatment setting. During the course of the exercise the therapist can make a general assessment of each patient, while the patient uses the exercise to *settle in*. By recalling the familiar life away from hospital and sharing this with unfamiliar people the patient achieves some degree of comfort and personal identity.
2. Sandra Watanabe, O.T.R., *Four Concepts Basic to the Occupational Therapy Process*, American Journal of Occupational Therapy (1968) XXII, 5, p. 439.
3. Half a sheet of construction paper makes a sturdy backing and allows each person to choose a colour that reflects his personality.
4. Work on the floor to encourage a free and relaxed atmosphere.

'Make a poster that illustrates your personality and life style, by selecting appropriate pictures from these magazines.

'Try to include pictures that show some of the following things about you (e.g., your attitudes and interests, likes and dislikes, characteristics, family, friends, job, ambitions, feelings, problems, reasons for being in hospital and so on). Be selective because it is impossible to illustrate every aspect of yourself'[5]	To increase self-awareness and encourage appropriate selection, discrimination and coordination of pictures from a wide range of possibilities
'Here are the magazines and scissors.[6] Let me know when you need the background paper[7]	To promote active participation and stimulate interest at the beginning of the exercise
'Let's complete the collage in twenty minutes'	Providing a set time in which to complete the task encourages organization in working. It also helps the overactive person control his need to be all inclusive

5. Analysis of the pictures selected will aid in the assessment of each person's perceptual and motor ability, mental state and life space.
6. To encourage communication and sharing, provide fewer scissors and glue pots than there are group members.
7. When working with patients with low self-esteem, who often reject activities for fear of looking foolish, present them with the scissors and magazines first of all and give them the paper and glue when it is needed. This eliminates the feeling and response of 'We're back at kindergarten,' that occurs when they are confronted with all these materials at once.

Besides making her own poster, the role of the
therapist is to clarify the task for those who don't
understand and to encourage discussion while
everyone is working

When the time is up ask, 'Does anyone need more time?'	To encourage each person to decide whether his collage is completed or not and to take responsibility for requesting more time
When all are finished, invite each person to tell the group about his collage. It is important that the therapist also talks about her own collage	To provide an opportunity to share personal information with other people and aid in the establishment and recognition of a personal identity. To provide a basis for conversation between individuals

Comments

Eavesdropping

Allow 1 hour

This is a technique concerned with increasing awareness both of other people and oneself. It exercises the skills of perception, observation and memory.

Recommended for these problems
— *poor memory*
— *poor perception*
— *low self-esteem*
— *poor self-awareness*
— *lack of interest in other people*
— *social isolation*

Stage of group development
The exercise is suitable for a group in which the members know one another fairly well but do not give one another support. It is good for a group with low morale.[1]

Synopsis
Each individual writes down everything he can remember about a group member who is out of sight. This person returns to the group and these observations are then shared and discussed.

Materials and equipment
Sheets of paper
Pencils.

Procedure

Invite the group members to sit in a small circle on the floor	This assists a sense of cohesion within the group and a relaxed atmosphere
Ask them to pass around the paper and pencils, keeping one of each for themselves	This encourages a decision to actively participate

---

1. This is an excellent exercise to use when group or individual morale is low. The comments will, for the most part, be constructive and encouraging and result in the increased confidence and self-esteem of the participants. It should also be used in groups where the participants are very isolated, since it will encourage them to make some degree of contact with each other. This should result in an increased awareness of each other and more group cohesion.

Explain the exercise as follows:

'One person will volunteer to leave the room	This allows each individual to decide whether he wishes to expose himself to comments from other people
'While he is away, the remainder of the group will each make a list of the things[2] they can remember about him (e.g., physical appearance, clothing, likes or dislikes, personal strengths, etc.)	This encourages increased awareness of other people. It means one has to think carefully about the person and recall facts, events, feelings, etc. pertaining to him
'When everyone has written all they can, the person outside the room will return and join the circle'	
Each participant will then be invited to read out what he has written down	This promotes direct verbal comment from one person to another. It provides an opportunity for experiencing the giving and receiving of supportive observations and constructive criticism
Discussion should be encouraged[3]	This encourages comparison of perceptions and an opportunity to clarify the feedback

Discussion topics
— Do the comments compare or contrast with how each person sees himself?
— Why are the comments and observations of others important?
— In what situations does one normally receive comments about oneself from other people?
— How does each person deal with the comments?

Comments

2. This requirement can be made more specific, e.g., 'write down all the problems that you remember he has.' At the same time, the person absent might list what he considers his problems to be. This would promote discussion, comparing and contrasting what the group see as problems and what the individual sees.
3. This exercise can be followed by a discussion of the types of things observed. It often happens that as the exercise progresses, the comments change from concrete observations of clothing, etc., to more abstract recollections of personality.

Likes and dislikes

This is an exercise in self-awareness and communication.

Recommended for these problems
— *social isolation*
— *difficulty talking in a group situation*
— *poor self-awareness*
— *low self-confidence*

Stage of group development   This is an exercise which enables an unfamiliar, incohesive group to get to know one another and begin to interact.

Synopsis   It requires that each person list the five things they like most and the five things they dislike most on opposite sides of a piece of paper. This information is then used as a basis for discussion.

Materials and equipment
Sheets of paper
Pencils
Erasers
Room with a table and chairs.

Procedure

Invite the group members to sit around the table	To promote a sense of security and purpose (the solid table ensures a definite distance between the people)
Ask them to pass around the pencils and paper, keeping one of each for themselves	To encourage a decision on the part of each person to participate actively
Then give the following instructions: 'Label one side of your piece of paper with the word *Likes*. Then turn it over and label the other side with the word *Dislikes*	
'Under the appropriate heading write the five things you like most and the five you dislike most[1]	To encourage self-awareness through the process of evaluation and discrimination. The lists compiled are usually factual and relate to recent events in each person's life

'You have ten minutes in which to do this	To provide a time limit within which to work and encourage each person to apply himself to the task
After this time the sheets of paper will be redistributed amongst the group so that no one has his own[2]	This allows the shy person to describe himself through someone else
'Each person will have an opportunity to read out what is written on the sheet of paper he holds, so that the group can try to guess who wrote it and discuss the contents'[3]	To promote increased awareness of each other as interesting and unique individuals To encourage verbal expression and interaction The puzzle element makes the exercise more stimulating

Comments

---

1. There are many possible variations. The following are just a few examples:
   Things you like doing, things you dislike doing (to assist awareness of how the person spends his time), *Ways in which you behave towards other people, which they like or dislike* (to aid self-awareness and evaluation of the effect of one's behaviour upon others), *Identify problems that you have and list possible ways of dealing with them* (to encourage objectivity and realistic constructive thought). Role play some of the alternatives to provide an opportunity for the person to experience and/or practise some of his ideas, as well as receive feedback on the solutions.
2. The lists could be put in a hat and each person asked to choose one as he takes his turn. This variation is useful when there are distractable or anxious people in the group who would be reading the list given them rather than listening to the discussion.
3. Where problems, feelings or aspects of behaviour are being identified, it is important that the discussion include constructive alternatives, contributed either by the group members, the therapist or, more usefully, by the individual himself.

Allow 40 minutes

Store

In this exercise each person's positive qualities are identified and used as a form of barter in order to purchase another person's positive qualities.

Recommended for these problems
— *low self-esteem*
— *poor self-concept*
— *egocentricity*

Stage of group development
This is a good exercise for a loosely knit group which is not very cohesive and whose members can only tolerate fairly superficial interaction.

Synopsis
The positive qualities of the merchant's personality are goods which may be purchased at the store by a buyer. As money, the buyer must use the positive qualities of his own personality. The store's *Board of directors* judge the exchange.

Materials and equipment
None
Use a large, comfortable room.

Procedure

Explain the exercise as follows:
'In this game called *Store*, one person plays the merchant. In his store he has some of his positive personal qualities for sale (e.g., cheerfulness, honesty and tidiness). Any person may go into the store and buy the qualities that are up for sale. However, the buyer must offer a tempting selection of his positive qualities to the merchant in exchange for his purchases[1]

To give participants an opportunity to assess themselves

---

1. This exercise can be varied to encourage players to recognize positive personal qualities in other people, In this case the buyer identifies qualities he sees in the merchant that he would like to buy and the merchant calls his price by identifying qualities in the buyer that he feels are desirable and which he would like to have in exchange.

'Before the transaction can be closed the merchant must take it to the store's *Board of Directors* for approval. Approval is given after a brief discussion during which the *Board* assesses whether the trade of personal qualities is a fair one

To give the two people some objective comments on how valuable their qualities are, as seen by others

---

'The *Board* will be made up of all the other players'

This involves the audience so as to keep their attention on the exercise

---

Encourage other members to take a turn at being merchant and buyer

---

Discussion topics — Discuss what personal qualities were traded and why.
— Discuss self-esteem and how it influences one's life.
— Discuss the importance of looking for positive personal qualities in other people.

Comments

CONVERSATION SKILLS

Who stole the cookie* from the cookie jar?

Allow 5–10 minutes

This exercise is a rhythmic *warm-up* technique.

Recommended for these problems
— *poor concentration*
— *psychomotor retardation*
— *social isolation*

Stage of group development The exercise can be used successfully with most groups.

Synopsis It is a *theatre game* in which words are said in time to a clapped rhythm.

Materials and equipment Blackboard and chalk
Use a room that is spacious.

Procedure

Before the session starts, write the words to be spoken on the blackboard[1]	This is to assist anyone who has difficulty remembering them
Invite the players to kneel on the floor in a circle . . .	A circle enables everyone to see everyone else and promotes a sense of wholeness
and to number off to the right. The leader is usually Number One[2]	Encourage the players to speak up clearly, so that everyone can hear
Explain the game as follows: 'The leader claps his hands in a simple rhythm[3] which the rest of us imitate	To do this requires concentration, motor coordination and a sense of rhythm

---

* or Biscuit.
1. Words to be written up:
   'Who stole the cookie from the cookie jar?'
   'Was it you number . . .?'
   'Who me?'
   'Yes, you.'
   'Couldn't be.'
   'Then who?'
   'Number . . .'
2. If the players are familiar with the exercise the leader can be a group member.
3. Begin with a very slow and simple rhythm so that the speed of it can be increased later on in the game.

'Then when everyone is familiar with the rhythm the leader begins speaking in time to it, saying . . .

'Leader: "Who stole the cookie from the cookie jar? Was it you number four?"[4]	The exercise becomes more difficult at this point, demanding greater concentration and psychomotor coordination
'Number Four: "Who me?" Leader: "Yes, you" Number Four: "Couldn't be" Leader: "Then who?" Number Four: "Number Ten"[5]	This provides an opportunity to practise quick verbal interaction Since the players do not know which one of them will be called next they need to remain alert
'Number Ten: "Who me?" Number Four: "Yes, you" Number Ten: "Couldn't be" and so on'	
If at any point one of the players fails to speak in time to the rhythm the game stops, and starts again with this particular person as the new leader	The person who is finding the exercise difficult assumes a more influential position in the group . . .
He begins his own rhythm and then in time to it says, 'Who stole the cookie from the cookie jar?' and so on.	that allows him to set a slower pace
As the players become proficient the speed of the rhythm can be increased	This will have the effect of intensifying the need to concentrate and react quickly

Comments

---

4. Any number from amongst the group members may be used.
5. Or any other number that a group member has.

Word circle

Allow 15–30 minutes

This is an exercise to improve a person's ability to think and speak clearly, especially when he is surprised. It can be used as a *warm-up*.

Recommended for these problems
— *difficulty speaking clearly*
— *difficulty thinking quickly*
— *poor concentration*

Stage of group development
This is an appropriate exercise for a rather apathetic group of patients who will not or cannot do a physically active exercise.[1]

Synopsis
The exercise takes the form of a non-competitive game, during which a player has to call a predetermined number of words, all beginning with a particular letter of the alphabet. There is a time limit imposed, which is directly proportional to the size of the group and dependent upon an object being passed around the circle from person to person. The ultimate goal of the game is to call out the same number of words as there are people playing.

Materials and equipment
A small object, e.g., book
Small carpeted room.

Procedure

Instruct the players to sit on the floor in as small a circle as possible	This encourages close association with another person and gives a sense of unity to the group
Explain the rules of the game as follows: The *leader* of this game sits in the centre of the circle while an object is being passed around from player to player at an even speed	Sitting in the centre of the circle makes the *leader* an integral part of the whole group. Passing the object helps each person to concentrate and remain involved
The *leader* closes his eyes and claps his hands once. He then announces a letter of the alphabet, excluding X and Z	Two decisions are involved here, when to clap and what letter to call. The *leader* is also required to speak out clearly

---

1. This is an excellent game and the authors recommend that it is played frequently as proficiency increases with practice.

'When he claps, the person in the group to touch the object last, calls out a predetermined number of words[2] beginning with the announced letter'

This encourages fluency in both thinking and speaking. The skills of concentration, retention and recall are used, as well as the ability to select appropriate words. Increased vocabulary may also result

The number of words required should be small at first and increased as the players become more proficient

Achieving success in calling the words will improve a person's confidence and decrease his anxiety about failing. This will ultimately enable him to become proficient

'Meanwhile the object is still being passed around the circle and if the *caller* fails to list off the required number of words before the object returns to him he replaces the *leader* in the centre of the circle

This imposes a time limit in which to complete the task and enables the person to experience a situation requiring quick thinking. If a person fails to think of the correct number of words he is not punished, but instead changes his role from that of player to that of leader

'If the *caller* succeeds then he remains in his place and the game continues with the original *leader*'[3, 4]

Comments

2. The words can be nouns, verbs, adjectives, adverbs, etc.
3. To encourage a sense of responsibility invite the group, as a whole, to see that the rules of the game are adhered to. They should also decide on the number of words to be called at any one time (bearing in mind that this number be low enough to provide a sense of achievement and high enough to be challenging).
4. Variations may include: words that rhyme or words in a particular category (e.g., countries, animals).

Balloon debate

This is an exercise in public speaking.[1]

Recommended for these problems
— *inhibited in self-expression*
— *confused thinking*
— *difficulty making decisions*

Stage of group development
A group that is just beginning to enjoy a sense of cohesiveness will benefit most from this exercise.

Synopsis
The group imagines that they are seated in the basket of a hot-air balloon which is sinking. Although each of them is a famous person, the only way to save the balloon is to lighten it. Thus, all but one of the passengers must jump overboard. In a short speech, each person puts forward the reasons why he should be the one to be saved. Voting is based on the content of the speech, and the person with the most votes is the winner.

Materials and equipment
Pencils and paper
Use a familiar room that is quiet.

Procedure

Invite everyone to sit in a circle	To promote awareness of the group as a unit and of the individuals in it
Pass around the paper and pencils, inviting everyone to keep one of each	To encourage a decision on each person's part to actively participate

---

1. This exercise is suitable for *videotaping*, particularly if the purpose of the exercise is to help patients practise more effective speaking. The replay can then be used to look at such things as:
   — whether everyone spoke loudly enough,
   — whether they spoke to the group as a whole or only to a segment of it,
   — whether they were able to keep everyone's attention,
   — whether they were able to emphasize their ideas with gestures and facial expression.

Explain the exercise as follows:
'Imagine that we are all seated in the basket of a
hot-air balloon which is sinking rapidly. The only way
to prevent the balloon from crashing is to lighten it.
All but one of us must jump overboard. However,
since each one of us is a famous person, we are given
the opportunity to put forward any reasons why we
should be the one to be saved'

'Firstly, decide which famous person you would like to be; you can be anyone either living or dead[2]	This part of the exercise provides each person with an opportunity to make a decision and be imaginative
'In the next three minutes, write down all the arguments you can think of why you, as this famous person, should be saved'	To assist an individual to relate his assumed identity to reality, and to encourage the use of his abilities to remember, reason and be innovative
When the three minutes are up, invite one person to be the *secretary*. His job will be to write down the assumed name of each person as he speaks	This is an opportunity to involve a quiet person in an active role
Ask each person in turn to stand up and introduce himself to the group, using his assumed identity, and share the reasons why he considers he should be saved[3]	To provide an opportunity for delivering a brief speech
Encourage everyone else to listen attentively and to make notes if they wish	To assist concentration and recall
'When everyone has spoken, a vote will be taken and the person who receives the most votes will be the winner	
'The *secretary* will record the votes'	The quiet player now has an opportunity to take a leadership role in the group
At the time of voting the therapist should remind each player that he only has one vote which he should cast for the group member whose speech contained the most persuasive reasons. Players may not vote for themselves	This exercises decision-making
When all the votes have been cast, the *secretary* reads out the results	

---

2. The therapist should be prepared to give suggestions to those patients who do not have any ideas (see Suggestions at the end of the exercise).
3. The therapist may need to restate the reasons presented if they are very garbled.
   Not only will this make the person's presentation more successful, but it will also give him the feeling that he has been understood.

Discussion topics

— What feelings did players experience while standing up in front of everyone and giving their speeches?

— How do players feel and react in other situations where they are expected to contribute to the conversation?

Suggestions for 'Ballon debate'

The characters chosen can be famous politicians, comedians, singers, film stars, writers, inventors and sportsmen. They can be people who are alive today or who have died.

Queen Elizabeth II	King Henry VIII
Albert Einstein	Darwin
Julie Christie	Shakespeare
Henry Kissinger	Caesar
Idi Amin	John Lennon
Captain Cook	U Thant
Yehudi Menuhin	Robert Redford
Margot Fonteyn	Scarlet Pimpernel
Napoleon	Elvis Presley
Johann Sebastian Bach	John Wayne
Florence Nightingale	

Comments

Describe a diagram

Allow 1 hour

This is an exercise to illustrate the difference between two types of communication,[1] that is, between a monologue and a dialogue.

Recommended for these problems
— *difficulty initiating conversation*
— *poor concentration*[2]
— *poor judgement*[3]

Stage of group development
This exercise is excellent for a group in which the members are still unfamiliar with each other. No feeling of group cohesion is needed.

Synopsis
One person is asked to describe a diagram precisely. The group members listen to the description and individually attempt to reproduce the diagram on paper from the instructions given. No questions or gestures are allowed. A second diagram is then described but this time both questions and gestures are allowed. The group members are encouraged to discuss the two exercises comparing and contrasting them.

Materials and equipment[4]
Tables
Chairs
Diagram cards (see sample diagram ideas at the end of the exercise)[5]
Sheets of paper approximately the same size as the diagram cards, e.g., 8 cm × 13 cm
Pencils
Erasers
Sharpener.

---

1. The exercise is suitable for *videotaping*. Afterwards the replay can be used to look at and discuss specific difficulties that the participants experienced in trying to communicate. The tape will also help participants recall how they felt at any one time.
2. This is an exercise where all the participants are involved actively, all the time. It is suitable, therefore, for patients who have a short attention span and who need constant stimulation if they are to maintain any contact with reality.
3. Patients with temporal lobe lesions are likely to find this exercise very difficult. It is important that the therapist makes an accurate assessment of how complex the diagrams should be for the participants to achieve success and yet be stimulated.
4. To promote a sense of responsibility, invite the group to prepare the room and materials.
5. To increase self-esteem, invite the participants to design their own diagram cards.

Procedure

Ask the group members to sit around the table(s)	
Pass around the pencils and paper inviting each person to take one of each	This encourages each person to be responsible for his participation
Explain the exercise as follows: 'One person in the group will be given a card on which there is a diagram. Only he may look at it	This provides an opportunity to experience leadership
'He will describe the diagram slowly and as accurately as he can . . .	This encourages succinct, logical description, attention to detail, accurate judgment and concentration. It exercises the ability to perceive a shape and translate that perception into words
'while the rest of the group attempt to reproduce this diagram on paper from the instructions they hear.	This exercises the capacity to form a concept from auditory stimuli and reproduce this concept in graphic form. It assists concentration, attention to detail and accurate judgement
'No one may ask any questions. Try to be aware of any reactions or feelings you may have while doing the task	This promotes self-awareness especially related to feelings in a situation where the communication is one-way only. The therapist should observe the reactions so that she can use her observations to stimulate discussion
'On completing the drawing there will be an opportunity for you to discuss your reactions and ascertain how accurate your diagram is before we proceed'	This provides an opportunity for heightening awareness of the feelings experienced during the task and will focus attention on the problems and/or frustrations inherent in one-way communication
Ask if there is a volunteer who wants to describe the first diagram and give him the card (if there is no volunteer the therapist takes this role)	This transfers leadership from the therapist to the participants
When the first part of the exercise has been completed explain the second part as follows: 'Another person will describe a different diagram	This enables more than one person to experience being the leader
'Again each group member will attempt to reproduce this from the description but this time you may ask questions	This will promote two-way communication. The participants will ask questions to clarify points and so experience the feelings that result from successful communication
'The person giving the description may answer the questions and gesticulate to clarify the points he is making	This provides an opportunity to practise using gestures in addition to words

'Again try to be aware of your reactions and feelings while doing this exercise'

This encourages the participants to be more aware of themselves in a particular situation

When the task is completed to the satisfaction of the group members, invite them to discuss the exercise

Discussion topics Compare and contrast the two exercises considering the following:
— What feelings were evoked?
— How important were the gestures in aiding communication?
— How do these experiences (in communication) compare with our daily lives?
— Why is it important to be able to ask questions?
— Are there situations in your daily life which illustrate the two types of communication?

Comments

SOME SUGGESTIONS FOR DIAGRAMS

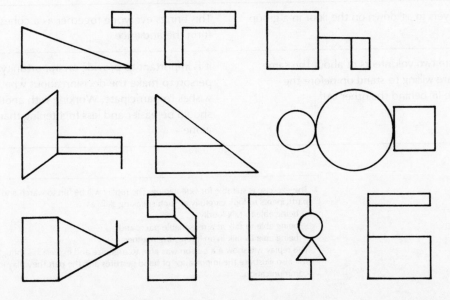

Hand puppets

Allow 5–10 minutes per pair

This is an exercise to help a person talk easily and with more confidence in a group situation. It may also stimulate a greater awareness in him of one of the nonverbal aspects of communication, i.e., hand gestures.[1]

Recommended for these problems
— *difficulty talking in a group situation*
— *poor speaking skills*
— *difficulty thinking quickly*

Stage of group development
This exercise is most successful with a group in which the participants are fairly comfortable with each other.

Synopsis
This is a *theatre game* in which two people stand up, one behind the other, before an audience (made up of the rest of the group). The front person delivers a short speech, while the back person, placing his arms forward so that they appear to belong to his partner, uses his hands to augment what is being said.

Materials and equipment
None
Use a familiar and preferably carpeted room.

Procedure

Invite the players to sit down on the floor in a group	This brings everyone together as a cohesive unit to form the audience
Ask if there are two volunteers of about the same height, who are willing to stand up before the audience, one (*B*) behind the other (*A*)[2]	It is important to provide an opportunity for each person to make the decision about whether he wishes to participate. Working with another person should be easier and less frightening than doing it alone

---

1. The exercise is suitable for *videotaping*. The replay will be fun to watch and will enable the participants to look carefully at such speaking skills as:
    being able to talk loudly
    being able to talk at a reasonable pace, and
    being able to talk in an interesting manner.
   The replay will show if a person was able to organize and express his thoughts clearly. It will also illustrate the importance of hand gestures and the part they play in communication.

Explain the exercise as follows:

'A holds B close to his own body, by clasping his hands behind B's back, and . . .	Standing very close together will assist them to work more easily as one unit
'B puts his arms forward so that they look as though they belong to A (see illustration)'	

'A then delivers a short speech to the audience . . .[3]	Encourage A to talk spontaneously even if it is only for a very short time
'and his partner (B), using his hands, gesticulates in order to augment what is being said'	To work as a team, B will have to concentrate on what A is saying
Encourage the audience to participate with laughter, applause, etc.	This is very important as it provides positive support and encouragement for the two players
'Then, keeping the same positions, the procedure can be reversed, i.e., B gesticulates and . . .	
'A makes up a monologue to fit the motions of B's hands'[4]	In this way A is encouraged to speak impulsively, without being self-conscious

2. An alternative is to have one pair of players carrying on a conversation with another pair. As the number of people on *stage* increases so the amount of attention focused on each individual decreases. This may encourage more people to participate.
3. If A does not have any ideas the therapist should have a few suggestions prepared. (See Suggestions at the end of the exercise.)
4. Stress that the sentences do not have to form a logical story as long as they fit the gestures and actions. This should help to introduce an atmosphere of comedy and enjoyment into the exercise.

Suggestions for 'Hand puppets' — A politician giving an election speech
— A person giving the vote of thanks after a lecture
— A demonstrator in a store, selling an all-purpose chopping utensil
— An announcer giving a weather forecast or reading the news
— Telling a story
— One person interviewing another who has just climbed the highest mountain in the world, or eaten the most hamburgers
— Two women having a conversation about some clothes they have purchased

Comments

Mystery objects

This is an exercise in tactile perception.

Recommended for these problems
— *low self-esteem*
— *difficulty with social interaction*
— *poor sensory awareness*
— *difficulty staying in touch with reality*

Stage of group development
This exercise is useful for a group whose members have difficulty talking to one another.

Synopsis
It takes the form of a *theatre game* in which a player is given a small article to hold behind his back. Then using his sense of touch he tries to answer questions about the article, and guess its identity.

Materials and equipment
Container
50 small articles.

Procedure

Beforehand invite all the players to bring a number of small articles, collected from home[1] to the activity	To encourage a sense of responsibility and involvement in the group's activities
Prior to beginning the game, pass the container around for each person to place his contributions in, without revealing them to the others	
Then invite the players to sit down in a circle and ask if there is a *volunteer* willing to stand up in front of everybody	To provide an opportunity for a group member to take a risk in a warm supportive environment
Explain the exercise as follows: 'The *volunteer* stands with his back to the group and his hands behind him	

---

1. In-patients can be invited to bring articles from within the hospital setting, or personal belongings.

'The *leader*[2] takes an object out of the bag and places it in the hands of the *volunteer*

'He then asks the *volunteer* six or seven questions about the article[3] (e.g., "What shape is it?" "What size is it?" "How does if feel?" and amusing questions, such as "What colour do you think it is?" and finally "Do you know what the article is?")	To provide the volunteer with an opportunity to arrive at a decision using tactile discrimination and deduction
'The *volunteer* attempts to answer these to the best of his ability, without looking.' (As the group can see the article some of the questions and answers can be very amusing)	To improve tactile perception and verbal interaction related to an everyday object
After a given number of questions (e.g., ten), the *volunteer* is invited to look at the object before placing it back in the bag. He then returns to his place in the circle	So that he can compare his visual perception with what he sensed by touch
Encourage the audience to applaud and then . . .	To provide the group member with a rewarding and supportive conclusion to his turn

invite another *volunteer* to come forward.[4]

Comments

2. Once the therapist has demonstrated how the game is played, the position of *leader* can be taken by a group member.
3. Encourage seated group members to think of questions to ask as this will help them to feel more involved.
4. This exercise can be adapted for patients who are very withdrawn and isolated. If simple, everyday objects are used, the chances of success in identification are considerably increased.

Playreading

This is a technique of reading a play together to help the members give vent to suppressed feelings and to stimulate discussion about a shared experience.[1]

Recommended for these problems
— *difficulty expressing feelings*
— *difficulty talking in a group situation*
— *social isolation*
— *poor speaking skills*

Stage of group development
Do not use this technique with a larger group than ten, especially if the members' concentration is poor. The technique is suitable for either a newly formed group or a group who are fairly well acquainted.

Synopsis
A play is read with all members taking a part that suits them. Afterwards there is a discussion.

Materials and equipment
Copies of a play[2]
Magnifying glass (optional)[3]
Comfortable sitting area.

Procedure

It is important to have read the play beforehand	To be aware of long, short, easy and difficult parts
Read out the *Introduction* and/or *Stage set instructions*	To give everyone an idea of the type of play which they are about to read
Read out the description of the characters	To prepare them for choosing a part

---

1. The exercise is suitable for *videotaping*. The replay can be used to look at some of the specifics of speech such as loudness, clarity, tone, pitch and speed. Time could also be spent looking at whether the participants were able to use appropriate facial expression, gestures and other nonverbal behaviours to supplement their spoken parts.
2. Try to obtain enough copies of the play for half the number in the group, so that no more than two people have to share a copy.
   Plays can be obtained from – *Plays for the Living*, a division of Family Services Association of America, 44 E. 23rd St., New York 10018.
3. This is handy to have on hand for those who have lost their glasses or have difficulty reading because of medication.

Ask for volunteers for each part.
If members seem reluctant to choose parts, encourage the other group members to assist them in choosing appropriate parts

To give the reticent member some feeling of identity and to help him realize that he is a part of the group

When there are more members than characters instigate a *Prompter,* a *Soundman* and a *Stage director*[4]

Start reading the play as soon as this is done and if possible continue until the play is finished

To make best use of the initial interest shown in the play and to keep up the mood of the play

Discussion topics   — Discuss the feelings that the play aroused.
— Discuss the plot and message that the play had for them.
— Discuss the way the players became involved in their parts.
— Discuss seeing plays and movies in the community.

Comments

---

4. The position of *Stage Director* is suitable for an overactive, overtalkative member.

Simultaneous conversations

Allow 5–10 minutes

This is an exercise in self-assertion. It takes the form of a *theatre game*.[1]

Recommended for these problems
— *poor concentration*
— *lack of assertiveness*
— *poor eye-contact*
— *difficulty speaking spontaneously*

Stage of group development
The group members should be familiar enough with each other that they can all risk being assertive in a supportive environment.

Synopsis
Two players sit opposite one another and are assigned to be either *for* or *against* a designated topic. Then, at the same time and maintaining eye-contact, they talk at one another, *without* responding to any part of their opponent's monologue.

Materials and equipment
None.

Procedure

Invite two players to sit facing one another . . .	This provides an opportunity for volunteers to come forward
and to make eye-contact	To assist concentration upon the other person
The remainder of the group form the audience	To provide a sense of 'theatre'
Ask the audience to name a topic[2] (the more ridiculous it is the more amusing the exercise) . . .	To encourage a sense of involvement on everyone's part and promote enjoyment

1. The exercise is suitable for *videotaping*. The replay can be watched just for fun or to look at the specifics of being assertive. These would be such things as being able to maintain eye-contact, talk at a reasonably even pace, talk quite loudly, think quickly and creatively and not opt-out of the game in any way. The nonverbal behaviour of participants can also be observed. The therapist can help the players become aware of how to reinforce what they have to say by using appropriate body positions, gestures and facial expression.
2. In case the group is not forthcoming with any suggestions the therapist should be prepared with some alternatives (see Suggestions at the end of the exercise).

and assign[3] one of the players to be *for* it and the other to be *against*

Explain the exercise to the players as follows: 'The object of this game is to defend your assigned stand, using all the arguments you can possibly think of and to *avoid* responding to *any* of your opponent's monologue.[4] You do this by talking *at* one another simultaneously	To provide an opportunity for self-assertion and to encourage increased concentration and extemporaneous speech
'Try to keep looking each other in the eye all the time	To encourage the ability to follow one train of thought without being easily distracted
'The players will start speaking when I signal, and . . .	
'you, the audience are the *jury*	
'Listen carefully to their conversations and if either of them hesitates, answers his opponent's monologue, or stops speaking altogether, call out, because he is the loser'	To encourage concentration and a sense of participation on the part of the audience
The game then continues with either the loser being replaced by the person who noticed his mistake or another pair of players with the same or a new topic	To enable all the participants to have an opportunity of experiencing the exercise
A discussion at the end may be appropriate[5]	To assist self-awareness and expression of feelings evoked by the exercise

Discussion topics
— What did the group members think about the exercise?
— How did it make them feel?
— What does being assertive mean?
— How can a person be assertive?
— What nonverbal behaviours help a person be assertive?
— How does this exercise differ from normal interaction?

3. It may assist players who are not very self-assured if they are able to choose whether to be *for* or *against*. This is because it is often easier to defend something one believes in and has chosen to support.
4. As the players become more familiar with the exercise, encourage them to force their opponent to respond by such ruses as questions, gesticulations, laughter, etc.
5. During discussion it may be appropriate to point out that this game does not approximate normal conversation where it is always important to listen and respond to another person. However, the exercise may highlight some of the frustration that can be felt when one's conversation is ignored. It will also reinforce the importance of maintaining eye-contact when trying to keep another person interested in what one has to say and provide a chance to practise being assertive.

Suggestions for
'Simultaneous conversations'

Jellybeans	Garbage cans
Bottle tops	Politicians
Doughnuts	Clouds
Mini skirts	Cigarettes
Pornography	Milk
Highrise buildings	Log cabins
Gardening	Newspapers
Dates	Chewing gum
Comedians	Banana skins
Rubber bands	Secondhand Shoes

Comments

Soapbox debate

This is an exercise to help a person feel more comfortable when speaking in a group. It encourages decision-making and reasoning in a clear logical manner.[1] [2]

Recommended for these problems
— *difficulty speaking in a group situation*
— *low self-confidence*
— *difficulty making decisions*
— *difficulty formulating opinions*

Stage of group development
The exercise should be used at a stage in group development when the participants feel fairly comfortable with one another.[3]

Synopsis
This exercise takes the form of a modified debate. Each person, in turn, makes a decision *for* or *against* a set topic and then supports their decision with three reasons. No one else may voice his/her opinion until the speaker has finished and throws the topic open for debate.

Materials and equipment
Chairs around a table
Prepared slips of paper (or paper and pencils[4])
A container (hat, box, etc.).

---

1. The exercise allows each person to express opinions that he may have held when he was functioning healthily and when he relied on his own judgement. It involves short periods of concentration (while listening to the speaker) alternated with an opportunity for the expression of thoughts. It is, therefore, a useful exercise for listening, thinking and speaking.
2. The exercise can be *videotaped*. The replay can be used to look carefully at whether the participants were able to make decisions, formulate opinions and present their reasons clearly. Poor speaking habits such as mumbling, talking very softly, talking very loudly, talking very fast or in a very hesitant way will also become apparent. The observations made while watching the tape can form the basis for a discussion.
3. It is contraindicated for the physically overactive patient.
4. Decide whether you or the group members are to prepare the topics for discussion. This will depend on how inventive the group members can be in their choice of issues. If this task is given to the group members it may encourage them to show an active interest in community affairs (see Suggestions at the end of the exercise).

Procedure

Before beginning the exercise, list a number of controversial issues on separate slips of paper.[5] Word each one so that it can be answered by 'Yes' or 'No'. For example: 'Do you believe that there should be a minimum drinking age in pubs?'	The issues can be chosen to suit the group, but should relate to current events (as found in local/national newspapers). This will encourage contact with the world outside the hospital. Be aware that clear wording of each question will assist the speaker to think more clearly
Invite the group to sit around a table	This gives the group a comfortable 'boardroom' atmosphere
Explain the exercise as follows: 'Each person will have a chance to be on the soapbox	To raise self-esteem, as each person will be listened to by the group
'You will take a topic out of the hat . . .	This freedom of choice may discourage the suspicious person from thinking that the topic was specifically written for him.
'and decide whether you are *for* or *against* it	To give an opportunity for decision-making
'Read the topic to us, tell us whether you agree or disagree with it and then back up your decision with three reasons'[6]	This gives each person a structure around which to organize his thoughts and communicate them clearly
In this exercise, the therapist has two jobs: (1) maintaining the freedom of speech for the speakers when necessary and (2) restating clearly what the speaker has said (if he has combined his three points into one sentence or if he has rambled)	To show the individual he has the right to speak no matter how difficult it is for him To give him a chance to hear his thoughts clearly stated and to give him the positive feedback that he has been understood
When the speaker has finished open the topic for debate	This will encourage an interchange of ideas between two or more individuals who may otherwise find spontaneous conversation difficult
Move on to the next person after a maximum of ten minutes[7] [8]	To allow time for each person to take his turn

5. Issues which are non-threatening and of an impersonal nature are easiest for discussion. Select the types of issues in relation to the group's overall capability in handling them.
6. It may be appropriate to give each person a pencil and a slip of paper on which to note his points.
7. When there are verbose and/or hyperactive members, or if the group is large, it may be advisable to limit both the speaker's time and the open debate.
8. Do not distribute all the topics at the start, or you may find some people unable to listen to the speaker as they are concerned about how to defend their own topic best.

Discussion topics	— Why is it important to be able to make decisions?
	— What are some of the problems caused by being indecisive?
	— How easy or difficult was it to formulate opinions?
	— What happens in a conversation when everyone is in agreement?
	— What happens in a conversation when people have differing opinions?
Suggestions for 'Soapbox debate' topics	— Will it rain tomorrow?
	— Should cars be kept out of the city centre?
	— Is a welfare state essential?
	— Should cigarette advertising be banned?
	— Man must work to enjoy his leisure.
	— Is space research important?
	— The monarchy is essential for a democratic state.
	— Cars should be limited to one per household.
	— Strikes are more effective than bargaining.

Comments

Story, story

Allow 10–30 minutes

This is an exercise to help a person feel more confident speaking, without any preparation, to a group of people.[1]

Recommended for these problems
— *low self-confidence*
— *difficulty speaking spontaneously*
— *poor concentration*
— *poverty of ideas*

Stage of group development
This exercise is best used in a group that has developed some unity and where the members are actively participating to the best of their abilities.

Synopsis
This is a *theatre game* in which a group of players tell a story. Each player speaks in turn, trying to keep the story coherent and grammatically correct. If however, someone makes a mistake then the story stops while this particular player mimes his own death and then joins the audience.

Materials and equipment
None
Use a familiar room.

Procedure

Invite from four to seven[2] players to form a line . . .	This provides an opportunity for volunteers to come forward[3]
in front of the audience . . .	To promote a sense of *theatre*
and one person to be the *Director*[4]	

---

1. This exercise can be *videotaped*. The replay can be watched just for fun or to look more specifically at some of the difficulties participants encountered. These might be such things as not being able to think of anything to say, difficulty paying attention and not speaking audibly.
2. Since this exercise is dependent upon there being enough people to be both *story tellers* and *audience*, the number of *story tellers* should be no more than half the group.
3. Depending on the degree of response the therapist may need to encourage or even choose *story tellers*.
4. Initially it may be advisable for the therapist to take this role, thereby demonstrating how to direct the game and promote enjoyment. A withdrawn person might be encouraged to participate as the *Director's assistant* and select the speakers.

Explain the exercise as follows:

'The audience chooses a *hero* about whom the players are going to tell a story	This encourages audience participation
'The *Director* then says, "The *hero* of your story is . . ." and points to one of the players, who immediately begins to make up a story about the designated hero	This person is encouraged to speak spontaneously
'The player continues with his story until the *Director* points to a different player (the game is more entertaining if the switch occurs while the person speaking is in the middle of a sentence)	
'This person takes the story up where the previous speaker left off and so the game continues	
'The only rules are that the story must be grammatically correct and coherent	This means that the players need to listen very carefully as well as concentrate upon the *Director*
'It is the responsibility of the audience to edit the story, that is to listen for any grammatical mistakes, repeated words, etc., and as soon as they hear one to cry, "Die"	The continuous audience participation in this way requires concentration and active involvement in the game
'At this point the story stops,[5] while the player who made the error mimes his own death[6] and then joins the audience	To encourage self-expression and provide an opportunity to be entertaining
'The *Director*, repeating the last word that was spoken, points to another player and the story continues until one player is left'	To refresh the players' memories
This person concludes the story with a moral and is either applauded or asked to 'Die', depending on whether his moral is accepted or rejected by the audience	

5. The *Director* must remember the last word spoken.
6. It is best if the leader mimes a few examples of entertaining deaths before the game starts, stressing that the action should be exaggerated and funny. Encourage the audience to applaud the player when he finishes his mime.
We are aware that some therapists may view this part of the exercise as threatening and/or untherapeutic. Although suicidal thoughts or attempts are experienced by many patients, they are infrequently discussed in a group setting. This exercise does not presume to promote discussion about suicide: it merely attempts to encourage expression of death in a nonverbal and entertaining way. We recommend that the therapist assesses whether the group can cope with this but not to underestimate their ability or allow her own anxiety to be the deciding factor. In practice we found that the participants react to the exercise according to how it is presented.

The game can be continued with a new set of players and a new *hero*

Invite discussion at the end

Discussion topics — Discuss any feelings that were evoked by having to speak up in front of a group.
— Discuss the effect of audience participation, laughter and applause upon the story tellers.
— Discuss feelings evoked by miming death.

Comments

THE PLAYER WHO MADE THE ERROR MIMES HIS OWN DEATH

The chair

Allow 10–30 minutes

This is an exercise in spontaneous self-expression and social interaction. It takes the form of a *theatre game*.[1]

Recommended for these problems
— *anxiety*
— *lack of assertiveness*
— *difficulty speaking spontaneously*
— *low self-confidence*

Stage of group development
It is recommended that this exercise be done with a group whose members are well enough acquainted that they feel safe to improvise.

Synopsis
A player from the group initiates and develops a skit with an opponent who is seated in a chair. The purpose of the skit is to persuade the opponent to get up from his seat.

Materials and equipment
Chair
Use a familiar room that is quiet.

Procedure

Invite the players to sit in a large circle on the floor and to find comfortable positions	To encourage everyone to be relaxed and, thereby, make participation in the exercise easier
Create a *centre stage* by placing a chair in the middle of the circle and . . .	
ask is there a volunteer who would like to sit in the chair	To provide an opportunity for a member to choose to be the centre of attention
Explain the exercise as follows: 'The object of this game is to persuade the person in the chair to get up from it. You may use any means to achieve this, apart from moving the chair or physical force	

1. The exercise is suitable for *videotaping*. The replay will be fun to watch for all members. The participants will be able to view their abilities to speak spontaneously, to be assertive, or to be persuasive.

'Any player may approach[2] the person in the chair and . . .	To encourage spontaneous participation
'through his actions and/or conversation set the scene[3]	To provide an opportunity for self-expression
'The two of them converse until the seated player is finally persuaded to stand up	To assist the formation of a brief relationship with another person and to practise communication with him
'Other players may join in the conversation at any point if they wish to	This freedom allows individuals from the audience to support and encourage the players by spontaneously participating with them
'Once the seated player does stand up he re-joins the circle. His opponent, taking the seat, waits to be approached by another player who starts a new skit'[4]	To allow as many players as possible the chance to participate, especially those who are shy or self-conscious and require some encouragement
Audience participation should be encouraged at all times (i.e., laughter, applause, verbal encouragement, etc.)	To involve the maximum number of people

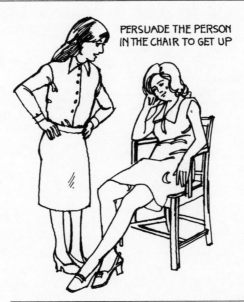

PERSUADE THE PERSON IN THE CHAIR TO GET UP

2. Unless the players are very self-confident, it is likely they will hesitate in coming forward initially. Since this is an exercise in spontaneity, we do not suggest that specific people are asked to participate, rather that the leader demonstrates the game using very ordinary familiar scenes (see Suggestions at the end of the exercise). In this way, the group members can be encouraged to feel safe enough to act out their own ideas.
3. For example: a player may approach the person in the chair walking like an old man and make a comment that sets the scene of a bus; or he may walk briskly and say, 'Good morning, madam. Is there a particular shoe that interests you?', thereby setting the scene in a shoe shop.
4. As the game continues, encourage the person in the chair to be more reluctant to give up his position. This will allow the players to be more subtle and skilful in their handling of the situation.

Suggestions for 'The chair'   Choose situations which are familiar, easy to enact and naturally require that one of the participants is seated. They should also lend themselves to comedy and improvisation.

— Buying a pair of shoes in a shoe store
— Two people sitting in a doctor or dentist's waiting room
— Finding yourself in someone else's seat at the theatre
— Travelling on the bus when a pregnant or heavily laden lady gets on
— Eating dinner at a restaurant and the waiter spills the soup
— Sitting in the cockpit of an aircraft that is about to crash
— Sitting on a park bench enjoying the sunshine

Comments

You really did it this time, Mabel!

Allow 15–30 minutes

This is an exercise in impromtu conversation and interaction.[1] It takes the form of a *theatre game*.[2]

Recommended for these problems
— *difficulty initiating conversation*
— *difficulty with social interaction*
— *difficulty being uninhibited*

Stage of group development
This exercise is only appropriate for a group that has been together for a while so that members are comfortable with one another and have gained some self-confidence.

Synopsis
Beginning with the words 'You really did it this time, Mabel!' pairs of players take it in turns to enact a conversation in front of the rest of the group.

Materials and equipment
None
Use a familiar quiet room.

Procedure

Invite the players to stand in a circle . . .	To facilitate a sense of cohesion and support amongst the members
with a *volunteer*[3] in the centre	To give the opportunity for an individual to express his self-confidence and a desire to actively participate

1. This is a difficult exercise and should only be done with adequate preparation with the group in the form of other *theatre games*.
2. The exercise can be *videotaped* and the tape replayed to watch the verbal and nonverbal interaction of the players. The replay can be particularly useful for observing the subtleties of interaction that occur since these will often indicate how a person relates to others during his daily life. These observations can then be used to form the basis for a discussion.
3. Demonstrate this exercise where possible, using either staff members (e.g., co-therapist/observer, students) or a fairly verbal group member as the first volunteer.

Explain the exercise as follows:
'The player A in the centre of the circle is a *neutral person*. That means he is not able to speak until spoken to and will be a partner in any scene that another player wishes to involve him in

'Player B, with a situation in mind approaches A, puts his hand on A's shoulder and says "You really did it this time, Mabel!" and follows it up with anything he wishes. For example "You really did it this time, Mabel, you broke Edna's brassiere"[4]	This requires the ability to create an impromptu situation as well as the desire to initiate a conversation
'A then replies in any way that he wishes and the two of them become involved in a dialogue'	To encourage creative thinking and spontaneous verbal interaction. The situations used may also necessitate expressing a variety of different ideas and feelings in relation to another person
A conversation develops from the initial exchange, providing the players cooperate with each other. If however, one of the players consistently negates a statement made by his partner the dialogue will quickly come to an end. For example, 'But Edna is only two years old'	
'As the conversation continues any other player C[5] may come forward with a different situation	
'He taps B on the shoulder in order to interrupt and terminate the dialogue between A and B and says, "You really did it this time, Mabel . . ."'	
'A leaves and rejoins the circle. B replaces A as the *neutral person* and C becomes B. The group is responsible for keeping up the flow of ideas and players involved'[6]	Telling the group this, stimulates them to be actively responsible for the continuation of the exercise
After a reasonable period of time the group can be invited to discuss their reactions to the exercise	To provide an opportunity to express feelings related to an experience common to all the participants

Comments

4. Scenes can be serious, ridiculous, real, fantasy, etc., and the more involved the players become in expressing their ideas and feelings to one another the better.
5. The sense of responsibility for maintaining a conversation or initiating a new one can be quite anxiety-provoking for both staff and patients. It helps to play the game frequently and to keep the dialogue fairly short so that players are involved on centre stage for only brief periods of time.
6. The therapist should be aware when a dialogue is beginning to lose vigour and be prepared to step in with a new situation if volunteers are not coming forward.

SELF-EXPRESSION

Action mime

This is an exercise to help a person express his ideas to others. It can be used as a *warm-up* technique.[1]

Recommended for these problems
— *social isolation*
— *low self-confidence*
— *poor concentration*
— *poverty of ideas*

Stage of group development
This exercise is valuable to use with any type of group, from a newly formed one to a cohesive and well integrated one.

Synopsis
It takes the form of a *theatre game* where the players take turns to perform an action mime, using a small article as a substitute for an imaginary one. The object of the game is to guess the identity of the imaginary article from the player's action mime.

Materials and equipment
Small articles, e.g., comb, book, box, ashtray, pencil, etc.
Use a familiar and quiet room where there will be no interruptions.

Procedure

Invite the players to sit in a circle	This enables each person to become more aware of the others. It also helps to unite the group
Place a small article, e.g. a comb, in the centre of the circle	

1. The exercise is suitable for *videotaping*. The replay will give each person a chance to see himself in action. This is an excellent exercise to videotape for those patients who are extremely anxious about the image they present.

Explain the exercise as follows:
'In the centre of the circle I have placed a comb. In turn[2] each of us is going to pick it up and, without words, use it in such a way that our action gives it a new identity. That is, we *must not* use it as a comb, but as something else. Allow its shape, size, weight and texture to stimulate your imagination, and the rest of us will try to guess what it is from your action'[3]

To provide an opportunity for each person to express himself and his imagination in a nonverbal manner

The game requires concentration and some spontaneity. A suitable action-mime will be immediately recognized and thus give the player a sense of achievement, whereas an inapt one will not be. The player can then be encouraged to try alternative and more realistic actions

---

'Once someone in the group has guessed the identity of the imagined object correctly place the comb back in the centre of the circle for the next person to pick up'

The physical action of picking up or putting back the object provides each person with an opportunity to indicate nonverbally that he is either ready to take his turn or finished with it

---

Continue until there are no more ideas forthcoming before substituting a different article or going on to another exercise

Do not change the article too quickly if you wish to encourage ingenuity and imagination

---

Comments

---

2. Once everyone has had a turn, it can be useful to allow individuals to volunteer to play, especially if they need opportunities to experience decision-making and risk-taking in a supportive environment.
3. If ideas are not forthcoming, the therapist and co-therapist should be ready to act as role-models, by taking a turn first. This demonstration will also help to clarify the instructions.

Movement
and sound circle

Allow 15–30 minutes

This is an exercise in self-expression, communication, and interaction. It can be used as a *warm-up*.[1]

Recommended for these problems
— *psychomotor retardation*
— *inhibited in self-expression*
— *limited body awareness*

Stage of group development
This is an appropriate exercise for a group in which the members find communication difficult.

Synopsis
This exercise takes the form of a game where one player, standing in the centre of a circle, initiates a repetitive movement and an associated sound (e.g., marching to the sound 'boom, boom, boom'). He then teaches his movement and sound to another player who attempts to imitate both of them as closely as possible. The two people exchange positions and the new player develops the learned *movement and sound* into a different *movement and sound* of his own making.

Materials and equipment
None
Use a familiar room that is quiet.

Procedure

Invite the group members to stand in a circle	This enables each person to see and, therefore, be more aware of everyone else
Explain the exercise as follows: 'One person stands in the centre of the circle[2] [3] and . . .	To provide a focus for the attention of the group members

---

1. The exercise is suitable for *videotaping*. The replay can be watched just for fun and will allow participants to see themselves creating uninhibited body movements and associated sounds.
2. If the game is being played for the first time, the therapist is advised to take this position in order to demonstrate the instructions he gives. If, however, the players are familiar with the exercise, ask if there is a volunteer who would like to be in the centre of the circle. This provides an opportunity for someone to demonstrate initiative.
3. If the players are hesitant to be the only person in the centre, because it means they are the focus of everyone's attention, it may be advisable to begin with two or even three people there. Each one of them teaches his own 'movement and sound' simultaneously.

'initiates a repetitive movement, and in conjunction with it – a fitting sound[4][5][6]	To provide an opportunity for self-expression in the form of repetitive physical activity and simple verbalization
'When the movement and sound have evolved to his satisfaction[7] . . .	
'he moves to stand in front of one of the players in the surrounding circle	To encourage awareness of others and provide an opportunity to make a choice from a selection of alternatives
'He teaches his movement and sound to this person[8]	To encourage communication
'The player being taught tries to imitate both the action and the sound as closely as he can[9]	To encourage interaction while concentrating upon another person To assist self-awareness, since both the individuals are receiving visual feedback and how their actions appear
'When the *teacher* is satisfied that his movement and sound have been learned accurately, the two players change positions	
'The new player takes his learned movement and sound into the centre of the circle where he allows them to develop[10] into a different movement and sound of his own making'	
He then teaches his own movement and sound to another player and so the exercise progresses	To enable everyone to take part in the exercise The random choice of who goes into the centre of the circle tends to increase the spontaneity and is less anxiety-provoking than waiting to go in a particular order

4. With some groups (e.g., those who find it difficult to cope with more than one idea at a time), simplify the exercise. Begin with the movements and include the sounds as the group members become relaxed.
5. Encourage the players to keep the actions large and the sounds simple and loud, since they are easier to imitate and tend to be more stimulating.
6. As the players become more proficient, they may be encouraged to introduce words and phrases instead of simple sounds. A question and answer situation may develop or even a continuing story.
7. Ideally the movement and sound should evolve naturally to suit the person in the centre of the circle. Therefore, the therapist must discourage him from stopping to think, fumble or wonder 'what shall I do?'.
8. If the whole group imitates the action and sound as it is being taught this will encourage both an enthusiastic and energetic response. It may also help to keep the energy level up during the evolution of new action and sounds and tend to give the central player encouragement and support.
9. Encourage the action and sound to be repeated over and over again until the player can imitate them to the best of his ability.
10. Develop, that is, by exaggerating or distorting the sound and movement.

After the exercise is over you may like to invite the group members to discuss their reactions briefly. This exercise is often used as *warm-up,* in which case discussion may be more appropriate at the end of the session

To encourage expression of feelings evoked by the exercise

Comments

The journey

This is a projective *warm-up* technique.

Recommended for these problems
— *anxiety*
— *social isolation*
— *difficulty talking to new acquaintances*

Stage of group development
This exercise enables group members to share their experiences and thus get to know one another better. It is helpful, therefore, for a fairly newly formed group.

Synopsis
It takes the form of a fantasy suggested by the therapist and is followed by an opportunity for each person to share the images which he experienced.

Materials and equipment
None
Room which is carpeted, quiet and free from interruptions.

Procedure

Invite the group members to form a wheel on the floor, by lying on their backs with their heads together in the centre, their legs radiating outwards	To encourage a sense of unity between the individuals
Suggest that each person close his eyes and tries to relax completely[1]	To avoid distraction from external stimuli and assist each person to become still, both physically and mentally – images will occur more easily in this state

---

1. If the participants are very tense or anxious the therapist may have to spend some time assisting the relaxation process. This can be done by teaching the participants deep breathing and/or how to systematically relax their bodies.

Give the following instructions:
'Imagine you are strapped firmly to the spoke of a
huge cartwheel. You feel safe and secure
(Pause)
'Very, very slowly the cartwheel begins to lift off the
ground
(Pause)
'It floats slowly up and up until it stops and hovers
about a hundred feet above the ground. You can
see everything below very clearly[2]
(Pause)
'Now the cartwheel begins to move forward very
slowly
(Pause)
'It is taking you to the land of your choice, some-
where where you have always wanted to go or return
to – a place of great happiness
(Pause)
'Now the cartwheel has brought you to your
destination. It hovers over this place so that you can
take it all in before you begin the descent
(Pause)
'Slowly, the cartwheel starts to descend, until it
hovers just a few inches above the ground
(Pause)
'Then it settles gently onto the ground and you have
landed. In your imagination get up from the cartwheel
slowly and look around you. Begin to explore the
area, seeing everything round about in great detail.
Perhaps there is somewhere specific in this place
you would like to go. Think about who you would
like to accompany you and in your imagination
explore this place with your companion
(Pause)
'When you have completed your fantasy trip sit up'
When everyone is sitting up invite them to form a
circle by turning around to face inwards

To promote a sense of well-being

To encourage the sharing of this experience with
another person

To allow each person to complete his fantasy in his
own time

Ask each person if he is willing to share . . .
— where he went in his fantasy?
— why?
— what it was like?
— who he chose to go with him?
— why he chose that person?
— what the two of them did together?
— what it felt like?

To encourage the sharing of good experiences and
feelings amongst the participants
To assist them to become more aware of each other
and themselves

2. Tensions may also be eased by such suggestions as 'The sky is clear and blue and in the
sunshine you feel warm and relaxed.'

Comments

Magic box

Allow 15–30 minutes

This is an exercise utilizing nonverbal communication. It may assist an individual to improve his concentration and memory.[1]

Recommended for these problems

— *poor memory*
— *poor concentration*
— *inhibited in self-expression*

Stage of group development

This exercise is best used with a small group of people; they need not be familiar with one another.

Synopsis

This is a progressive game that makes use of an imaginary box. Each player, in turn, receives the *box* and, on opening it, has to take out and use all the previously created *objects* that it contains. He then adds one of his own, closes the lid, and passes the box on.
This exercise could be used in conjunction with other memory exercises such as *Kim's game,* or *Find the change.*

Materials and equipment

None
Use a familiar room that is carpeted.

Procedure

Invite the group members to sit on the floor in a circle of less than ten[2] people	To form a small unit of people who will feel at ease working together
Designate a leader in each group[3]	
Explain the exercise as follows: 'The leader will mime an imaginary *box*; (its shape, size, weight, and texture, etc.) which he will produce and place on the floor in front of him	To provide an opportunity for creative self-expression

1. This exercise is suitable for *videotaping*. The replay will be fun to watch and will allow each person to see his ability to be creative and uninhibited.
2. The amount of information that each person has to memorize is directly proportionate to the number of people in the group. If the attention span of the participants is short, it is advisable that the group be divided into smaller units.
3. If the exercise is familiar invite volunteers to take the position of leader in the group.

'He will open it and invent a mime *object* which he will use in such a way that it's identity is obvious to the rest of us.	To encourage contact with reality by recalling the use of familiar objects and to practise communication
'Then he will place the object in the *box*, close the lid, and pass it on to the next person[4]	To enable each person in the group to participate
'This player will open the *box*, remove the imagined object and use it in the same or a different manner . . .	This part of the exercise requires memory, imagination and concentration
'then, placing it back in the *box*, he will invent his own mime *object* which he will use and place in the *box* too	
'Closing the lid he will pass the *box* on to the next player'[5]	To encourage interaction between the two people
The *box* continues around the circle with each person using all of the previously invented *objects* and then adding one of his own	As the game progresses, there is an increasing amount of concentration, memory and initiative required on the part of each successive person
When the *box* finally returns to the leader, he removes all the *objects* one by one, uses them and then throws them away	To symbolically conclude the game

Comments

---

4. If the players are at all confused, specify the direction in which they pass the *box* (e.g., 'Pass the *box* to the person on your right.').
5. The therapist (leader) may need to remind the participants to remember the size, shape and weight of the *box*, as well as the contents.

Seeing a sport together

Allow 10 minutes

This is an exercise to help a person develop his ability to communicate an idea nonverbally.[1] [2]

Recommended for these problems
— *inhibited in self-expression*
— *poverty of ideas*
— *low self-confidence*

Stage of group development
The exercise is appropriate to use with a group whose members can benefit from mutual support.

Synopsis
This is a *theatre game* in which one team pretends to be watching a particular sport. The other team tries to identify the sport.

Materials and equipment
None
Use a spacious, carpeted room.

Procedure

Invite the players to divide into two equal teams.[3]
(Call the teams *A* and *B*)

---

1. A variation of this exercise is 'Eating a food together'. The team decides what type of food they are going to eat and then mime the act of preparing and eating it. Again this is done with each person working independently, but at the same time. Side-coaching includes such instructions as:
   smell the food
   put it in your mouth
   chew it
   feel its texture
   taste it
   swallow it, and then react with a sound to what you have just swallowed.
2. The exercise is suitable for *videotaping*. The replay can be watched just for the fun of it or it can be used to see what players were able to mime really effectively and why. What was it about their nonverbal communication that was innovative? Sometimes after watching a tape players may wish to do the exercise again to try out and practise new ideas. This can also be taped so that participants can then see whether they were able to effect any changes.
3. See reference to teams in the chapter entitled *Some basic concepts*.

Explain the exercise as follows:
'One team (e.g., *A*) takes the *stage* while the other team (in this case *B*) forms the audience and sits down

Participants on Team *A* decide amongst themselves on a particular sport[4] they are going to watch	This gives each team member an opportunity to give ideas and cooperate with the others in coming to an agreement

'Then, with each person working independently but simultaneously, the team members imagine they are watching that sport being played, and show their reactions in mime

'Team *B* watches the action of team *A* and try to guess the sport they chose'

Side-coaching[5] can be given by the therapist or a group member to assist the performers

'The teams then change places and Team *B* takes the *stage*'

Comments

4. The therapist should have a few ideas prepared in case the teams need suggestions.
5. Examples of side-coaching:
   watch the event being played far away
   watch it as it gradually comes closer and closer
   'see' the event with your head, with your hands, with your feet, and now with your whole body
   'see' it a hundred times larger than it is.

Painting to music

Allow 1 hour

This is a projective exercise to assist self-expression.

Recommended for these problems
— *poor self-awareness*
— *difficulty expressing ideas*
— *difficulty differentiating and expressing feelings*

Stage of group development
This exercise works well with a group of people who are acquainted with each other but need some means of expressing themselves in a group setting.

Synopsis
The group listens to a short piece of music several times. Each person then creates a painting to express the images or feelings that were evoked by the music. Afterwards everyone is invited to share his experience with the other group members.

Materials and equipment
Records or taped music[1]
Record player or tape deck
Sheets of paper, at least 40 cm × 50 cm
Water colour paints
Paint brushes of assorted sizes
Water containers
Newspaper
Overalls (optional)
Use a room with enough working space to promote a relaxed atmosphere.

Procedure

Invite everyone to sit in a circle, finding a really comfortable position	To assist each person to listen attentively to the music
Explain the exercise as follows: 'I am going to play a short extract of music through twice[2]	Clear, concise instructions tend to reassure those who are fearful of new experiences

1. For Suggestions refer to the end of the exercise.
2. It is not necessary to identify the music until the end of the exercise. This should encourage the expression of spontaneous rather than preconceived ideas and feelings.

'As you listen to it, try to be aware of what it makes you think of and how it makes you feel	To encourage self-awareness and concentration
'Then, in your own time . . . collect some paper, paints, etc., and try to put your reactions to the music down on paper, in the form of a painting	
'No doubt, we shall all experience the music differently; some of us may respond to the rhythm, others to the feelings or images aroused within ourselves[3]	To give reassurance and encourage each person to feel safe enough to express his reactions, even if they are different from that of the person next to him The therapist should observe how each person reacts
'I shall continue to play the extract until everyone has completed their painting and . . .	To enable reluctant participants to join in later on[4]
'then there will be an opportunity for each person to explain his painting if he so wishes'[5]	This will provide an opportunity for each person to share his reactions with the others
Encourage discussion, by using one's own observations and assisting the group members to use theirs	To increase awareness of one's self and others, and to encourage the giving and receiving of comments

Suggestions for 'Painting to music'

(a) Musical Selections suitable for stimulating a variety of emotional responses

Air for the G String	Bach
A Night on a Bald Mountain	Moussorgsky
Ave Maria	Schubert
Ecossaises	Beethoven
Latin American Symphonette	Morton Gould
Moonlight Sonata: (First movement)	Beethoven
Peer Gynt Suite No. 1: (Hall of the Mountain King)	Grieg
Peer Gynt Suite No. 1: (The Death of Ase)	Grieg
Piano Concerto No. 4 in G Major (First movement Bars 1–29)	Beethoven
Rite of Spring (Part I 'Adoration of the Earth')	Stravinsky
Scheherazade Suite: (First movement)	Rimsky-Korsakoff

3. Patients whose ego-boundaries are diffuse have difficulty discriminating between what is real and what is unreal and may, therefore, find this exercise rather anxiety-provoking. To help overcome this, the therapist is advised to use very descriptive music (see list of Suggestions) and to concentrate initially on the images rather than on the feelings aroused. She should also give assistance and encouragement to anyone requiring it.
4. With some groups it may be advisable to set a time limit. Do not be too concerned if someone does not wish to participate – it is likely he/she will when he/she sees the others involved and at ease.
5. Our experience with this exercise has shown that:
   (a) it tends to provide the very quiet person with an opportunity to express himself
   (b) the underlying feelings evoked in people are often similar, although their symbolic portrayal of the feelings may be different
   (c) the most withdrawn people are often the most perceptive

Scherzo No. 1 in B Minor, Opus 20	Chopin
Slavonic Dance No. 2	Dvorjak
Symphony No. 5 in C Minor: (First movement)	Beethoven
The Sorcerer's Apprentice	Dukas
William Tell Overture: (Finale)	Rossini
Violin Concerto in D Major: (Second movement Bars 1–20)	Mozart
Xerxes (Largo)	Handel

(b) Musical Selections suitable for stimulating the imagination

A Night on a Bald Mountain	Moussorgsky
Dance of the Hours	Ponchielli
Finlandia, Opus 26	Sibelius
Nutcracker Suite	Tchaikovsky
Peer Gynt Suite	Grieg
Pictures at an Exhibition	Moussorgsky
Romeo and Juliet Overture	Tchaikovsky
Symphony No. 6 in F Major ('Pastoral'), Opus 68	Beethoven
The Planets, Opus 32	Gustav Holst
The Seasons	Glazunov
The Vltava (Moldau)	Smetana

Comments

Self-portrait

This is an exercise in self-awareness and expression of feelings.

Recommended for these problems
— *poor self-awareness*
— *distorted body image*
— *difficulty differentiating and expressing feelings*

Stage of group development
The exercise is only appropriate when the group members have developed some degree of trust for one another.

Synopsis
Self-portrait is a technique during which each person in the group has his body outlined on a large sheet of paper. He is asked to paint within the outline to show how he feels today and is then invited to discuss the painting that results.

Materials and equipment[1]
Roll of 1 m wide paper
Water colour paints
Large paint brushes (e.g., 2·5 cm decorator brushes)[2]
Water containers
Water
Overalls
Felt pens
Newspapers
Masking tape
Use a large room with a sink unit in it and preferably no other furniture.

Procedure

Instruct each person as follows:
'Tear off a sheet of paper which is taller than yourself

The gross movement occurring tends to be tension reducing, which helps to prepare the person for freer movements when he is painting. An estimation of his own height is required

---

1. To promote a sense of responsibility, ask some or all of the group members to collect and return the materials needed, to prepare the room and to assist the less able participants.
2. To promote more spontaneity, provide larger paint brushes and reduce the time allotted for the portrait painting. This will also give additional time for discussion.

'Place this sheet of paper on the floor and lie on it, finding the position in which you are most comfortable and entirely relaxed	This encourages each person to relax and be calm. The therapist can assess each person's ability to follow the instructions
'Let me know when you are comfortable' Using a felt pen, draw around the first person who says he is comfortable, making an outline of his body	To encourage self-awareness and decision making
Invite this person to take the marker and draw around another person who says he is ready, and so on until each person has been outlined[3]	This task requires coordination and physical contact with another person. It may also increase awareness of body image through the sense of touch
Continue with the following instructions: 'Show how you feel, right now, by painting inside your own outline	This allows each person to express how he is feeling, graphically, and encourages him to search and identify the emotions inside him
'Use different colours for the different feelings you are experiencing	More than one feeling may be expressed by saying this
'Do *not* depict the clothes you are wearing	To discourage a concrete response
'Try to be finished in fifteen minutes'	This is to encourage uninhibited expression by each person and aid in the therapist's assessment of the ability to complete a task within a given time. The therapist should also observe such aspects as colour choice, manner of application and interaction
When the time allowance is up invite each person to explain the feelings he has portrayed in his painting	To assist the person to communicate his feelings verbally using the nonverbal material as a reference
Encourage discussion about the portraits by the group	This is to develop awareness of other people and their feelings, and encourage the participants to check the accuracy of their perceptions

Comments

---

3. If the group is large or the attention span of the members short, ask them to choose a partner and outline each other. This will ensure that the outlining part of the activity takes a shorter period of time.

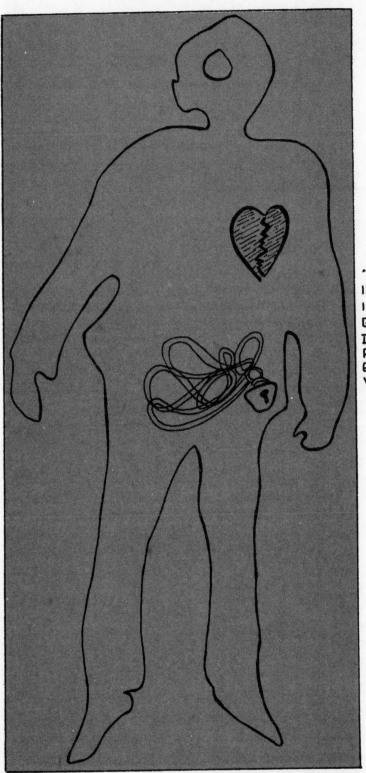

"THIS SHOWS A LARGE EMPTY AREA IN MY HEAD, AND MY STOMACH IS TIED UP IN KNOTS, PADLOCKED BUT I CAN'T FIND THE KEY... I FEEL DETACHED FROM MY FAMILY... I FEEL I DO EVERYTHING IN A MECHANICAL WAY"

SOCIAL INTERACTION

Body X's and O's

This is a *warm-up* technique. It involves the participants in simple gross physical movement through which they become more aware of one another and the concept of team work.

Recommended for these problems
— *psychomotor retardation*
— *anxiety*
— *social isolation*

Stage of group development
This exercise is helpful as a *warm-up* technique and for a group containing many isolated members.

Synopsis
It is based on the pen and pencil game of *X*'s and *O*'s.[1] Replacing the two opponents are two teams; replacing the grid drawn on paper is the same configuration made by placing tumbling mats on the floor[2] and added to the game is a coordinator. The object of the game is for three members of one of the teams to succeed in forming a straight line running in any direction through the grid.

Materials and equipment
Large area
Nine tumbling mats or chairs.

Procedure

Ask the energetic or anxious members to help you arrange the mats on the floor in three rows of three	This enables them to channel their anxiety or energy into constructive activity
Explain the exercise as follows: 'This game is similar to *X*'s and *O*'s. Is there anyone who does not know that game?	Relating the game to one that is familiar will help ease the fears of the more anxious players
Explain the object of the game for those not familiar with it: 'Instead of using paper we are going to use these floor mats and instead of two players, we are going to use two teams'	

---

1. *Naughts and crosses.*
2. Substitutes for tumbling mats could be squares of cardboard, chalk lines on the floor, or chairs.

If there is an uneven number of players, ask one person or a volunteer to be the *coordinator*[3]	This provides a non-physical leadership role for a person who is showing considerable psychomotor retardation or who is afraid to participate actively
Divide the group into two teams.[4] Call one '*X's*' and the other '*O's*'. Then ask each team to number off, i.e., from one to the number of people the team contains. This allows each player in the team to be paired off with a player in the other team with the corresponding number	Having one specific opponent may help to stimulate a competitive feeling towards that person and a relationship of friendly rivalry
'The *coordinator* is going to call out a number. The two players of that number will leave their respective teams and choose a mat	
'Two more numbers will be called out in succession and the players will compete to line themselves up to form three in a row and thus win the game for their team'	
Encourage the players to plan their strategy together and to cheer their team members on	This need for strategy brings the team members together physically and may give the isolated and withdrawn person a feeling of belonging

Comments

---

3. If the number is even, ask one of the team members to take this position.
4. See description on Formation of Teams in the chapter *Some basic concepts*.

Geography

Allow 10 minutes (minimum)

This is a *warm-up* technique. It is an exercise which assists a person to think more quickly, to concentrate and to practise immediate recall.

Recommended for these problems
— *poor concentration*
— *low self-esteem*
— *difficulty thinking quickly*
— *poor memory*

Stage of group development
A group that is meeting for the first time can attain some degree of cohesion from this exercise. However, it is also enjoyable and useful to do with a group at any stage of it's development.

Synopsis
Each person in turn says the name of a geographical place. The name he chooses must begin with the last letter of the geographical name that his predecessor chose.[1]

Materials and equipment
Use a room with chairs or a carpeted floor.

Procedure

Invite the group members to sit in a circle	To unite the group physically
Explain the exercise as follows: 'The game begins with one person saying the name of a place (e.g., *London*). The person seated to his left will then give another geographical name beginning with the last letter of the previous word (if we follow the example, then the place name must begin with *N* e.g., *New York*) and so the game continues around the circle	To be able to take his turn, each player must concentrate on what the previous player says, assimilate what he heard and then express his own actual contribution clearly
'No names may be repeated	This means that as the game progresses more and more names have to be remembered

---

1. This exercise is contraindicated for a group containing excessively active patients, or for patients for whom recall is so difficult that participation would be ego-deflating.
   People who do not speak English well can achieve success at this game, as they are not limited to English names only.

'However, if a person cannot think of a name, anyone may give him a clue in the form of a question (e.g., "What is the largest city in America?" Then he will remember *New York*)'

It is important, therefore, to encourage helpful communication between the group members and provide an opportunity (within the rules) for the restless person to participate when it is not his turn

Change to another exercise when you see signs of the first person becoming restless

Since this is a *warm-up* activity, it is best to stop while everyone is still interested and participating actively

Comments

Introductions

This is a *warm-up* exercise. It offers an opportunity to practise conversing with one person and then to express what one has learned to a group of people.

Recommended for these problems
— *social isolation*
— *low self-esteem*
— *poor conversation skills*
— *withdrawal*

Stage of group development
This is an ideal exercise for a group containing several new members, or for one in which the participants are particularly isolated and withdrawn.

Synopsis
The group divides up into pairs and each pair becomes acquainted with one another through conversation. Then, each person in turn, introduces and describes his partner to the remainder of the group.

Materials and equipment
A comfortable room where simultaneous conversations can be carried on without conflicting with each other.

Procedure

Explain the exercise as follows: 'In order to get to know each other better, we are each going to take turns to describe and introduce one other person to the group	The purpose of the exercise is explained in order to allay the fear of the unknown often held by new members
'Choose a partner with whom you feel most comfortable[1]	To eliminate some of the awkwardness in communication
'Move to a quiet spot in the room and say to your partner, "Tell me all about yourself." Collect as much information as he is willing to tell you. At the same time, he will be trying to learn all about you. In ten minutes, we will reform into a large group'	The competitive element in this exercise stimulates rapid two-way conversation and motivates interest in the other person. This time limit gives a work-oriented approach to the exercise

1. If the group members are quite self-assured, suggest that they choose the person they know least, but whom they would like to get to know, as a partner.

In ten minutes say, 'Your ten minutes are up. Please move into a large circle'	To physically unite and thereby create some cohesion in the divided group
When everyone is seated ask, 'Who would like to begin to introduce his partner by name and by description?	To give an opportunity for an individual to be assertive Being described by another person and hearing someone else describe oneself often reaffirms one's self-concept
Continue encouraging each person to take his turn when he feels ready to do so	When a person is introduced by someone else they tend to give more details about that person that otherwise would have been withheld out of modesty

Discussion topics — What feelings did each person experience while doing the exercise?
— Within each pair, how did the conversation go (i.e., did both participate equally, or one more than the other)?
— What social situations do you find yourself in where this type of conversation would be both appropriate and necessary?

Comments

Name game

This *warm-up* technique helps new members learn the names of other people in the group and provides each person with an opportunity to share something about himself. It also exercises concentration and memory.[1]

Recommended for these problems
— *poor concentration*
— *poor memory (recognition, retention and recall)*
— *difficulty talking to new acquaintances*

Stage of group development
It is a good exercise to use when working with a group which contains several new members.

Synopsis
This is a progressive *theatre game* in which each person introduces himself by name to the group and then shares something personal. Having done this he then tries to remember the names and personal contributions of all the people preceding him. If he cannot do this, the game begins again.

Materials and equipment
None
Use a room large enough for everyone to sit in a circle and be comfortable.

Procedure

Invite the group members to sit in a circle

Explain the exercise as follows:
'We are going to start today with a *theatre game* to help improve our concentration and memory. It will give us a chance to practise the art of introducing ourselves to another person and will help the new members learn our names

An explanation of the purpose of the exercise may help to allay any anxiety the participants feel

---

1. The exercise is suitable for *videotaping*. Watching the replay will provide each person with an opportunity to look at himself and his own behaviour more objectively. Specifically, the tape will show any habits participants have which make communication difficult or impossible (e.g., avoiding eye-contact, mumbling, speaking very softly, not paying attention, etc.). Once the habits have been identified each person is in a position to start learning more appropriate and effective ones.

'One person begins by introducing himself to the person on his left, saying "Hi, my name is X." He then tells that person something about himself[2]

This encourages a person to make specific contact with another person. This gives an opportunity for the group to begin learning something about each other's lives

'The person he is addressing then repeats what he has heard from X, and turning to the person on *his* left, introduces himself and gives a personal fact. And so it continues around the circle until the last person, who must recite all the names and facts, tells them to X.

'If at any time one of us cannot remember either a name or fact correctly then the game will start again at the beginning[3]
'The game is finished when everyone has had his turn'

This is so that the person who has difficulty remembering has another opportunity to learn the names

To start this exercise the therapist may either ask for a *volunteer* or designate someone, bearing in mind that since the game is a progressive one the last person to play has to remember considerably more than the first[4]

Discussion topics[5]
— What does it feel like to be in a room full of strangers?
— Why is it important to remember a person's name?
— Discuss the importance of being able to share personal facts when talking to another person.
— Discuss the importance of paying attention to a person's replies if one is interested in continuing the conversation.

Comments

2. Initially invite group members to share superficial facts about themselves, such as 'What is their favourite kind of food?', or 'What do they like doing most in their spare time?'. If the group members know one another well then this exercise is an excellent way to help them start sharing facts of a more personal and insightful nature, such as 'What problem brings you to this group?'.
3. Go back to the person who started and play the game exactly as before with each person sharing the same personal fact.
4. Cf. *Magic box*.
5. Since this game is primarily a *warm-up* technique it is likely that discussion will not follow it immediately, but after other exercises have been used.

Allow 5–10 minutes or 1 hour

Pass the ball

This is primarily a *warm-up* technique to provide personal introductions and assist name-learning. However, it can be extended to form an exercise in direct communication between participants.[1]

Recommended for these problems
— *withdrawal*
— *social isolation*
— *difficulty talking to new acquaintances*

Stage of group development
This is an excellent exercise to use as a *warm-up* for a group of people who are particularly quiet or withdrawn and do not know one another.

Synopsis
One person in the group passes the ball to another person and at the same time offers some verbal information about himself to the recipient.

Materials and equipment
Chairs (if the participants are unable to sit on the floor)
A ball (choose a large and light one if possible).

Procedure

Invite the group members to sit down in as small a circle as possible[2] [3]	This tends to provide physical closeness between group members and makes passing the ball across the circle easier
Place the ball in the centre of the circle and explain the exercise as follows: 'One person in the group will pick up the ball and give it to another person saying: "My name is . . ." The recipient, in turn, will give the ball to a third person saying: "My name is . . ." and so on	This involves the simultaneous actions of making physical contact with a chosen person and introducing oneself to him. Eye-contact and clear diction are encouraged

1. This exercise is suitable for *videotaping*. The replay can be used to show participants how they converse with one another and, more specifically, to identify potential communication problems (e.g., avoiding eye-contact, talking very softly, answering questions in a vague or indirect way, reluctance to share personal information, etc.). If problems are identified, these can form the basis for a discussion.
2. To provide an outlet for restlessness, make the circle larger. Then ask the participants to walk across the circle and give the ball to the person they have chosen.
3. To stimulate the motor senses (e.g., reflexes, muscle coordination and control), rather than intimate interpersonal contact increase the size of the circle. Then ask the participants to stand up and either throw or bounce the ball to one another when they speak.

'If, at any time, you do not wish to participate, then place the ball back in the centre of the circle	This provides an opportunity for opting out and the decision to do so is expressed nonverbally
'Anyone else may pick up the ball and continue with the exercise	
'When everyone has said their names several times, the sentence will be extended to include the recipient's name, i.e., "My name is . . . , your name is . . .", each time you pass the ball on	This improves the skills of recognition and recall. The associated physical contact acts as an added stimulus for those whose attention span and/or contact with reality is poor
'Now that you have learned everyone's name, when you pass the ball on, tell the recipient something about yourself, prefixing your statement with his name'[4]	This encourages the participants to share information about themselves
The exercise can be progressed stage by stage to include such topics as 'Now tell the recipient how you are feeling today'[5] [6]	This encourages the identification and expression of feelings in a direct and specific manner
The exercise could be concluded in the following manner: 'Finally, you can ask the recipient of your ball a question. He may answer you and then he can turn to another person with a question'	This promotes conversational exchanges between people but in a very structured way. It encourages the use of initiative and an awareness of other people

Discussion topics
— Why is it important to be able to share information about ourselves with other people?
— Why is it sometimes difficult to talk directly to a person?
— How do we avoid talking to people?

Comments

---

4. By sharing information in this way, new members joining a group are provided with some cues for further conversation.
5. In a smaller group members will get to know and trust one another more quickly than in a larger group.
6. As therapist you can decide what information will be helpful for the players to share with one another. Suggestions can also be elicited from the group members themselves.

Rhythm circle

This is a *warm-up* technique designed to assist group members to learn each other's names. The exercise will also help improve concentration, psychomotor coordination and sense of rhythm.

Recommended for these problems
— *social isolation*
— *poor concentration*
— *psychomotor retardation*
— *difficulty staying in touch with reality*
— *aphasia*

Stage of group development
This exercise is good for an incohesive group in which the participants do not know each other's names and are mutually disinterested.[1]

Synopsis
This is a *theatre game* consisting of a rhythmic sequential action coordinated with the calling of a person's name.

Materials and equipment
None.

Procedure

Ask the group members to kneel on the floor in a circle and then in turn to introduce themselves by name	The circle formation means that each person is within the vision of every other person
Demonstrate the rhythm as you give the instructions	To make the exercise easier to learn
Start by giving the following instructions: 'We will learn the rhythm first. To the count of six and using both hands . . . Slap your knees, twice (*one, two*) Clap your hands together, twice, (*three, four*). Snap your fingers, once with the right hand and once with the left hand, (*five, six*)	This requires concentration, coordination and a sense of rhythm
'We shall repeat the sequence from the beginning many times, trying to maintain an even pace'	This will help those whose concentration and immediate recall is rather poor

1. This is a good introductory exercise to use when new members join a group.

Continue practising until everyone can remember the actions and do them in time with one another. (The speed must be relative to that of the slowest person)	To reinforce the learning and promote a sense of individual and group achievement
'Now we have learned the actions, at the same time as everyone snaps their fingers, one player will call out his own name twice	This part of the exercise can be used to encourage each person to speak up loudly and distinctly
'We must all help to keep the rhythm going and . . .	Encourage the group members to be supportive of the caller, so that if he becomes muddled he can join in with the rhythm again
'while everyone snaps their fingers again, the same player will call out the name of another person twice	Using a person's name necessitates recognizing that person and making eye-contact with him
'The named person than takes over, firstly calling his own name twice and then that of yet another person (always in time to the finger snapping part of the rhythm) and so on'[2][3]	The repetitive nature of the game should assist the people to learn and remember each other's names

Comments

2. As practice tends to make the participants more proficient, this exercise can be successfully used on a regular basis.
3. This exercise is contraindicated for overactive patients as it is too stimulating.

Allow 10 minutes   # Salad

This is a *warm-up* technique which encourages body contact and concentration.

Recommended for these problems
— *apathy*
— *poor concentration*
— *psychomotor retardation*
— *difficulty with social interaction*

Stage of group development
Use this exercise at the beginning of any group in which the members have great difficulty communicating with one another and in which the general mood is one of lethargy.

Synopsis
Two players exchange seats when their *names* are called, while the caller attempts to sit in one of their vacated chairs.

Materials and equipment
Chairs in a circle
Have one less chair than the number of people in the group.

Procedure

Have each person choose a vegetable[1] [2] [3]

Explain that the game will begin with one person standing in the centre of the group. He will call out two vegetables and those two people must exchange places. He will try to sit in a seat vacated by one or other of them. If he succeeds, the person left standing is the next person to call out two vegetables. The caller also has the choice of calling out 'Salad', in which case everyone must change places

Success at this game requires a fair amount of concentration and quick movements

1. For people whose concentration is very poor allow each person to write the vegetable he has chosen on a piece of paper and then pin it to his chest. An alternative to this would be to list the vegetables chosen on a blackboard, as a reference list for the centre person.
2. Vegetables, fruits, flowers, etc., can be chosen for variety.
3. Every person should choose to be a different vegetable, i.e., no duplication.

Discussion topics — While the players are catching their breath, and before the next exercise a light-hearted discussion could be started about why individuals chose to be represented by their particular vegetable.

Comments

The matchbox is . . . ?

This is an exercise to develop the capacity to be observant and use words that are descriptive. It can be used as a *warm-up* technique.

Recommended for these problems
— *poor sensory awareness*
— *difficulty talking in a group situation*
— *difficulty staying in touch with reality*

Stage of group development
This exercise could be used with a group of very withdrawn patients to help them to stay in touch with their immediate situation and begin to communicate. If the exercise is used in this way the time allowance should be extended until the level of participation indicates that progression to another exercise is appropriate.

Synopsis
An article is passed around the group and as each person receives it he is invited to contribute one thing towards it's description.

Materials and equipment
Small objects such as a pencil, ashtray, key, vase, jar, etc.
Use a small familiar room.

Procedure

Invite the group members to sit in a circle

Explain the exercise as follows:
'I am going to pass a small *article*, (e.g., a matchbox) around the group[1]

'When each person receives it, he is invited to describe something about the *article*[2] before passing it on to the next person

To improve observation skills and to encourage the individual to say what he sees, or feels
This not only enables everyone to participate but the process of handing the object on encourages each person to relate to his neighbour

---

1. These articles can be collected beforehand or each person can be asked to produce something he has on him at the time.
2. With patients whose thought processes are very slow it is sometimes advisable to stimulate ideas by suggestion (e.g., as to shape, size, smell, texture, weight and use). This may be done as you give the instructions or may need to be given as coaching to each person in turn.

'The object of the game is to describe as many aspects of the *article* as we can without repetition'

To encourage greater concentration and originality

Continue passing the same *article* around until all possibilities have been exhausted and then invite a group member to introduce a new *article*

This stimulates the generation of a wide variety of observations, necessitating some creative thinking. Inviting the group members to make personal contributions may encourage a greater degree of interest and participation

Comments

Kim's game

The purpose of this exercise is to improve an individual's perception and memory, particularly in relation to objects. It takes the form of a competitive game.

Recommended for these problems
— *poor memory*
— *poor concentration*
— *apathy*
— *difficulty staying in touch with reality*

Stage of group development
This is an excellent exercise to use with a group who are not physically active and have a short attention span. It can be used as a *warm-up* exercise.

Synopsis
A tray of common objects is presented for the participants to look at; and after a short period of time, this tray is removed from sight. The players attempt to recall as many of the objects as they can.

Materials and equipment
Tray
Small common objects[1]
Pencils, paper
Room with table and chairs.

Procedure

Invite the participants to sit around the table and each[2] take a pencil and paper	To provide an opportunity for each person to be physically involved in the exercise
Explain the game as follows: 'I shall place a tray with 25[3] objects on it, in the middle of the table	
'You will have four minutes to look at the tray and memorize the objects	To encourage concentration, attention to detail and memorization

1. Objects that represent different aspects of life outside the hospital are useful for in-patients, as they provide contact with reality.
2. This game can be played by individuals, pairs, or teams according to the needs of the participants. For example, if they are very isolated then have them play in two's or three's since this will necessitate the interaction of one person with another and the sharing of ideas.

'The tray will then be removed and each of you will write down as many of the objects as you can recall

To practise the skill of immediate recall

'I shall then bring back the tray for you to check your answers'

To enable each person to measure his level of achievement

Discussion topics
— What methods are there to help us remember things and people's names?
— In what situations is a good memory important?

Comments

---

3. The number of objects on the tray should be varied according to the mental state of the participants. It is better to start with a low number of objects and increase the number each time the game is played, so as to provide a sense of accomplishment and improvement amongst the participants. This may in turn increase their motivation.
To provide a sense of involvement and responsibility, the therapist may wish to invite some of the players to put together their own trays of objects and in turn present them to the group. This provides an opportunity for the individual to use his initiative and also may assist the therapist in her assessment of him.

Baseball* quiz

Allow 45 minutes

This is a fairly active and yet intellectual exercise. It firstly promotes group cohesion through team rivalry and secondly raises an individual's self-esteem by rewarding him for the knowledge he has in a particular field of interest.

Recommended for these problems
— *low self-esteem*
— *psychomotor retardation*
— *social isolation*

Stage of group development

This exercise can be altered to suit two different types of groups: (1) a small group whose members are inhibited and have poor concentration (use this exercise as written), and (2) a large group whose members have good concentration, interest in others and some self-confidence (use the variation in footnote 1). It is a useful exercise when the group contains members who need physical activity to promote communication and yet will not participate in any technique which appears to be childish.

Synopsis

The exercise takes the form of a *baseball game*. One team *pitches* questions[1] while the opposing team members take it in turns to *bat* by answering a question which will score a *run* for their team.

Materials and equipment

Three more chairs than the number of group members
Blackboard, chalk and
Book(s) of quiz questions.

Procedure

Ask the group to help arrange the chairs to form a *baseball diamond*.[2] On the *pitcher's* mound put enough chairs for one team. Leave a row of chairs along the sidelines for the other team. Divide the group into two teams

The physical activity may present an opportunity for the anxious person to relieve his tension. It may also help stimulate the withdrawn members

---

* Baseball is a North American game. It is quite similar to Rounders.
1. A variation of this is to have both teams on the sidelines. The batting team members take it in turns to come up to homeplate to answer questions. The opposing team provides a permanent pitcher with a prepared list of questions.
2. See illustration for 'Baseball quiz'.

Describe the exercise as a *baseball game*:	Relating the mechanism of the game to a familiar sport may help clarify your description of how it is played
'The first player comes up to bat and chooses a category (from the list on the blackboard) from which he is prepared to answer a question	
'The team on the *pitcher's* mound collaborate and decide which questions to ask the *batter*. If he answers correctly, he goes to *first base* (and moves on from there as his fellow team members answer their questions correctly)	
'If he is incorrect,[3] he is given two more chances before he strikes out and returns to his chair on the sidelines	
'Points are scored when a runner reaches *home plate*'	This may be an opportunity to involve a very reluctant participant as score-keeper
Ask the group members to suggest categories[4] in which they would be prepared to answer questions. Record these categories on the blackboard	An individual can experience some feeling of success when he is able to answer questions in a category that is very familiar to him
Put yourself on the team that is *pitching* and begin the game	To assist in the decision-making process a co-therapist could be on the other team

THE PITCHERS

3RD BASE

2ND BASE

BATTER

1ST BASE

3. The pitcher must know the correct answer to his question.
4. See Suggestions for ideas.

Discussion topics   Use any topic that arises from the questions or categories.

Suggestions for   Spelling   Animals
'Baseball quiz' categories   History   Flowers
                        Geography   Famous People
                        Science   Religion
                        Cooking   Politics
                        Sewing   The Sea
                        Music   Birds
                        Entertainment Rivers
                        Sports   Current Affairs

Comments

Allow 1 hour Newspaper quiz

This is a technique to stimulate interest in and awareness of current events. It also encourages team work.

Recommended for these problems
— *difficulty staying in touch with reality*
— *poor community awareness*
— *difficulty talking in a group situation*

Stage of group development
This exercise can be used with a variety of groups but, because of its competitive element it is particularly useful in fostering group cohesion.

Synopsis
The exercise takes the form of a competitive game in which each team has to hunt through a newspaper for the answer to a specific question.

Materials and equipment
1 complete daily newspaper for each team of three to four people
1 table for each team
Chairs
Paper
Pencils
Blackboard and chalk upon which a visual record of the results can be kept.

Procedure

Beforehand prepare a list of questions,[1] the answers to which will be found in the newspaper. Number or label the tables.

Invite the group members to form teams of three or four people, and sit one team to a table	To form a team requires making contact with other people

---

1. In preparing the questions consider these points:
   Should you choose information in large print if there are some group members who are on large amounts of medication and have blurred vision?
   Are the questions difficult enough to be stimulating, yet easy enough to provide a sense of achievement?
   Do you need to give hints on the location of the answer in the paper?
   Have you prepared enough questions? (Allow approximately one minute per question.)
   Does the members' knowledge of current events need to be expanded?

Give the following instructions:
'On your table you will find a number which represents your team, a complete copy of today's newspaper and some pencils and paper'

Ask if there are volunteers willing to be the *question master* or *score keeper*. The therapist may need to assist the volunteers	Being *question master* or *score keeper* can be a suitable role for someone who feels the exercise is beneath him or for someone who might otherwise remain uninvolved
'The *question master* will read out a question and . . .	This requires clear, distinct speech
'the first team to find the correct answer in the newspaper will receive a point[2]	To encourage a sense of competition and cooperative interaction between the members of each team. At this time the therapist can observe how each person participates within his team
'The *score keeper* will assign a point to the appropriate team and then the *question master* will go on to the next question	To provide an opportunity for responsibility and cooperation between the teams and the volunteers
'The winning team will be the one which obtains the highest number of points overall'[3]	To provide an incentive for maximum effort and participation

Suggestions for 'Newspaper quiz' questions
— What is today's weather forecast?
— What film is now playing at the *Odeon*?
— Who won the football game last night?
— What store is advertising a Winter Sale?
— Which large building was reported to have burned down last night?
— What problem was Mr Brown writing about in *Letters to the Editor*?
— What is today's horoscope for those born in the beginning of May?
— On what page are *Jobs available* advertised?
— How much rent is being asked for the one bedroom apartment at 1611 Forge Street?

Comments

---

2. When there are more than two teams competing, it may be advisable that they write their answers down rather than call them out. The answers can be checked at the end of the quiz.
3. With some patients (e.g., children, adolescents, or chronically disabled adults), a prize for the winning team may be the additional stimulus which helps to maintain their interest and involvement.

TRUST

Allow 15–60 minutes # Blind circle

This is an exercise to increase a person's conscious awareness of other people, using senses other than sight.[1]

Recommended for these problems
— *egocentricity*
— *distorted body image*
— *fear of touching people*

Stage of group development
This is a good exercise for a group whose members need physical contact in order to feel closer to each other.

Synopsis
It takes the form of an identification game where each person closes his eyes and attempts to identify one person who has made various changes to his clothing and appearance.
It may be used as an extension to the *Blind Walk*.

Materials and equipment
None
Use a familiar room where there will be no interruptions.

Procedure

Invite the group members to stand in a circle, without touching one another, and facing inwards	To bring the group together
Explain the exercise as follows: 'Firstly, will everyone please close their eyes	
'I am going to guide one of you[2] into the centre of the circle and ask this person to make various changes in his clothing, (e.g., putting on glasses, taking off a jacket, wearing a hat, etc.)	To provide an opportunity for the use of initiative and to make it difficult for the participants to identify the person from his clothing alone

1. The exercise is suitable for *videotaping*. Watching the replay afterwards will show participants what occurred while their eyes were closed. The replay can also be used to assist each person recall his feelings during the exercise.
2. If the members are quite self-assured, an alternative would be to ask if there is a volunteer who would like to be in the centre of the circle (request a show of hands while everyone's eyes are closed and select one person).

'Only the person in the centre of the circle may open his eyes

'He will then silently stand in front of each one of you, in turn, and . . .	To encourage personal interaction through the sense of touch
'with your eyes closed you may like to try to identify him	To encourage physical contact with another person, especially the upper part of his body To increase the ability to recognize a person from his features rather than his clothes The therapist should observe the reactions of the participants and use these observations to assist any discussion that may arise later
'When everyone has had a turn at guessing you may open your eyes and see if your guess was correct'	To provide an opportunity for feedback with regard to the accuracy of perceptions
Encourage discussion in terms of any feelings or reactions that were experienced during the exercise, why some people guessed correctly and why some did not, and so on	To promote the sharing of experiences between the participants and to assist learning about oneself and others
Continue the exercise with a different person/ volunteer in the centre of the circle	Repetition will help to reduce anxiety and reinforce any learning that may have occurred

Discussion topics   — How did you feel during the exercise?
— How did you identify the players when you had your eyes closed?
— Did you like touching people?
— What part does touching play in relationships?
— Which of your senses did you use?

Comments

Blind run

Allow 10–30 minutes

This is an exercise to increase trust and self-confidence.[1]

Recommended for these problems
— *difficulty trusting people*
— *low self-confidence*
— *anxiety*

Stage of group development
This exercise should be done with a group who know one another quite well.

Synopsis
The exercise requires that a person walk or run across an oval (formed by the other participants) with his eyes closed. As he reaches the perimeter of the oval he will be caught, turned around and redirected.

Material and equipment
None
Use a large familiar room that has no furniture in it or where the furniture can be pushed to one side.

Procedure

Invite the group members to form an *oval*	This brings the group together as a visual unit and ensures that the distances walked or run are different
Ask if there is one person who would like to be in the centre of the oval. (Request that the gap he leaves is closed up)	To provide an opportunity for someone in the group to volunteer
Instruct this person as follows: 'Close your eyes tightly and turn around on the spot until you lose your sense of direction	To promote disorientation of this person with regard to his position in the oval and, therefore, increase the degree to which he must rely on the participants to look after him
'Then stop turning and walk forward trying to maintain an even pace	

---

1. The exercise is suitable for *videotaping*. The replay can be used to look at how each person was able to participate and particularly at how he used his body in relation to those around him.

'As your confidence increases, quicken your pace until you can run back and forth in a relaxed way	To encourage self-awareness and trust The speed at which the person moves will indicate the degree to which he feels he can rely on the group members
'Tell us when you have had enough'	To promote decision-making
Instructions to the group: 'When the volunteer (use his name) reaches the edge of the oval the person nearest him must catch him carefully, gently turn him around and redirect him across the oval again'	To promote a sense of responsibility for another person and encourage gentle physical contact with him To encourage concentration upon what is happening
Continue with another volunteer in the centre	To enable each person to experience the exercise if they so wish
Invite discussion at the end of the exercise	To assist the sharing of feelings, reactions and observations amongst the participants To increase self-awareness

Discussion topics — What is trust and how does it affect our relationships?
— What does it mean to be responsible for another person?
— How does it feel to be responsible for another person?
— How do we react in situations where we are dependent upon other people?
— How do we react to situations which are unfamiliar?

Comments

Caboose

This is an exercise involving physical contact, cooperation and the chance to experience a dependent versus a protective role.

Recommended for these problems
— *social isolation*
— *poor self-awareness*
— *depression*

Stage of group development
This can be used as a *warm-up* exercise but it should be done with a group that has developed some degree of trust. It is often useful when the group has become inactive (stale) in the middle of a session.

Synopsis
In form this exercise is a variant of *Dodgeball*. The players encircle two group members one of whom is *it* and the other is his *shield*. The players attempt to hit the person who is *it* below the knee with a thrown ball while he is being protected by his *shield*. If they are successful a new person becomes *it*.

Materials and equipment
A soft[1] large ball
Use a room that has plenty of free space.

Procedure

Invite the group to form a circle	The act of forming a circle requires some cooperation amongst the members, which may in turn stimulate greater awareness of themselves and others
Explain the exercise as follows: 'We are going to play a variation of *Dodgeball*'	To aid in comprehension by relating new experiences to familiar past experiences
'Instead of one, there will be two people in the centre of the circle	To provide a comfort to those people who dislike being the target of attention

---

1. Many older women are afraid of being hit by a thrown ball: a soft ball is less anxiety provoking.

'We will try to tag the first person (whom we will call *it*) with the ball while the second person (whom we will call the *shield*) will try to deflect the ball and thereby protect his partner[2]

To give an opportunity for each person to play one of two roles: firstly, guardian which is a protective role and secondly, the guarded, which is a dependent role
Once the individual has played a protective role and found it quite easy he will have more confidence in his protector when he is *it*

'When *it* is successfully tagged he is out. (To tag successfully the ball must hit *it* below the knees.) Then the *shield* becomes *it* and the person who throws the ball successfully, becomes the *shield*'

The successful individual is rewarded for a strategically planned and well coordinated shot with the honourable position of protecting someone else. This is in contrast to regular Dodgeball where there is no reward other than remaining on the team

As soon as any member of the group shows signs of restlessness, either change to another game or stop for a discussion

Discussion topics
— What was the difference between the two roles?
— What were the similarities between the two roles?
— What is teamwork?
— Is teamwork necessary during one's daily life?
— If so, why?
— What effects do the players feel after the physical exercise?

Comments

---

2. It is much more difficult to tag in this manner. Team cooperation is needed to pass the ball quickly between players in order to catch the unprotected *it* from behind. This has the effect of increasing concentration, interaction and cooperation between the individual group members.

Glossary of current psychiatric terms

This includes terms used in this handbook.

Accessible. 'Easy to get along with, talk to, or deal with: capable of being influenced or affected.'[1]

Acting out. 'Expressions of unconscious emotional conflicts or feelings of hostility or love in actions rather than words. The individual is not consciously aware of the meaning of such acts. May be harmful or, in controlled situations, therapeutic (e.g., children's play therapy).'[2]

Activation. 'Stimulation of one organ-system by another; the term stimulation is generally reserved for external influences only.'[3]

Active therapist. 'Type of therapist who makes no effort to remain anonymous but is forceful and expresses his personality definitively in the therapy session.'[4]

Activity. 'In occupational therapy, any occupation or interest wherein participation requires exertion of energy.'[5] See also Passivity.

Activity, group. 'In occupational therapy an activity in which several patients participate. Its chief value is it's socializing effect upon the mentally ill patients who are asocial.'[6]

Activity, socializing. 'In therapy groups, this term denotes the activity that brings an individual into interaction with other members of the group.'[7]

Affect. 'A person's emotional feeling tone and it's outward manifestations. Affect and emotion are commonly used interchangeably.'[8]

Affect, blunted. 'A disturbance of affect manifested by dullness of externalized feeling tone. Observed in schizophrenia, it is one of that disorder's fundamental symptoms, according to Eugen Bleuler.'[9]

Affect, flat. See Affect, blunted.

---

1. *Webster's Third New International Dictionary of the English Language. Unabridged* (1971) p. 11 Springfield: Merriam.
2. Frazier, S. H., Campbell, R. J., Marshall, M. H. & Werner, A. (1975) *A Psychiatric Glossary* p. 10 New York: Basic Books.
3. Hinsie, L. E. & Campbell, R. J. (1970) *Psychiatric Dictionary.* 4th edn p. 12 New York: Oxford University Press.
4. Freedman, A. M., Kaplan, A. I. & Sadock, B. J. (1972) *Modern Synopsis of Psychiatry* p. 749 Baltimore: Williams & Wilkins.
5. Hinsie & Campbell (1970) p. 13.
6. Ibid.
7. Hinsie & Cambell (1970) p. 14.
8. Frazier *et al.*, p. 11.
9. Freedman, A. M., Kaplan, A. I. & Sadock, B. J. (Eds.) (1976) *Modern Synopsis of Psychiatry/II, 2nd edn* p. 1280 Baltimore: Williams & Wilkins.

Aggression. 'A forceful physical, verbal or symbolic action. May be appropriate and self-protective, including healthful self-assertiveness, or inappropriate. Also may be directed outward toward the environment, as in explosive personality, or inward toward the self, as in depression.'[1]

Ambivalence. 'The coexistence of two opposing drives, desires, feelings, or emotions towards the same person, object, or goal. These may be conscious or partly conscious; or one side of the feelings may be unconscious. Example: love and hate toward the same person.'[2]

Anger. 'A strong feeling of displeasure and usually of antagonism.'[3]

Anomia. 'Difficulty in recalling the names of things, a variety of Aphasia,'[4]

Anxiety. 'Apprehension, tension, or uneasiness that stems from anticipation of danger, the source of which is largely unknown or unrecognized. Primarily of intrapsychic origin, in distinction to fear, which is the emotional response to a consciously recognized and usually external threat or danger.' It 'may be regarded as pathological when present to such an extent as to interfere with effectiveness in living, achievement of desired goals or satisfactions, or reasonable emotional comfort.'[5]

Apathy. Lack of feelings or affect; 'lack of interest and emotional involvement in one's surroundings.'[6]

Aphasia. 'Loss of or impaired ability to speak, write or to understand the meaning of words, due to brain damage.'[7]

Appearance. 'The look or outward aspect of anything; often refers to physical details such as facial features or expression.'[8]

Apprehension. When used by psychiatrists apprehension is almost invariably connected with the feeling of fear, anxiety, or dread. 'There is a tendency, however, to use more circumscribed expressions such as anxiety, in place of such a general term as apprehension.' The term can also be used to describe 'the intellectual act or process by which a relatively simple object is understood, grasped, or brought before the mind.'[9]

Appropriate. 'Specially suitable.'[10]

Asocial. 'Not social; indifferent to social values; without social meaning or significance.'[11]

Assertive. 'Characterized by self-confidence, determination, and boldness in asserting opinions or in otherwise making one's presence or influence felt.'[12] See also Self-assertion.

Assessment. 'The act of assessing: an evaluation.'[13]

---

1. Frazier *et al.*, p. 11.
2. Ibid., p. 13.
3. Webster (1971) p. 82.
4. Drever, James (1965) *A Dictionary of Psychology* p. 16 Harmondsworth: Penguin.
5. Frazier *et al.*, p. 16
6. Freedman *et al.* (1972) p. 753.
7. Wolman, p. 29.
8. *Webster's New World Dictionary of the American Language, College Edition* (1968) p. 70 New York: World Publishing Co.
9. Hinsie & Campbell (1970) pp. 59/60.
10. Webster (1971) p. 66.
11. Hinsie & Campbell (1970 p. 66.
12. Webster (1971) p. 131.
13. Ibid.

Assess, to. 'To analyse critically and judge definitively the nature, significance, status or merit of.'[1]

Attention and concentration. 'The aspect of consciousness that relates to the amount of effort exerted in focusing on certain aspects of an experience.'[2]

Attitude. The 'preparatory mental posture with which one receives stimuli and reacts to them.'[3]

Awareness. 'Mere experience of an object or idea; sometimes equivalent to consciousness.'[4]

Behaviour. 'The manner in which anything acts or operates. With regard to the human being the term usually refers to the action of the individual as a unit. He may be, and ordinarily is, acting in response to some given organ or impulse, but it is his general reaction that gives rise to the concept of behaviour.'[5]

Body awareness. See Body image.

Body image. The conscious and unconscious picture a person has of his own body at any moment. The conscious and unconscious images may differ from each other.

Body language. 'The system by which a person expresses his thoughts and feelings by means of his bodily activity.'[6]

Chemotherapy. 'The prevention or treatment of disease by chemical substances which, while effective against the pathogenic organism, have no harmful effects on the patient.'[7]

Cognitive. 'Referring to the mental process of comprehension, judgement, memory, and reasoning, as contrasted with emotional and volitional processes. Contrast with conative.'[8]

Communication. The 'transmission of emotions, attitudes, ideas, and acts from one person to another. The distinction is made between the "primary" techniques of communication common to all men such as language, gesture, the imitation of overt behaviour and social suggestion, and the "secondary" techniques which facilitate communication, as writing, symbolic systems including stop-and-go lights, bugle calls and other signals, and physical conditions allowing for communication such as the telephone, railroad and the airplane.'[9]

Communication, nonverbal. See Nonverbal interaction.

Communication, verbal. See Verbalization or Verbal technique.

Comprehension. 'Understanding, especially as opposed to mere apprehending or cognition.'[10]

1. Webster (1971) p. 131.
2. Freedman *et al.* (1972) p. 754.
3. Ibid.
4. Drever, p. 26.
5. Hinsie & Campbell (1970) p. 90.
6. Freedman *et al.* (1976) p. 1286.
7. *The Faber Medical Dictionary* (1975) Sir Cecil Wakeley (Ed.), revised by Bate, J. G. p. 89 London: Faber & Faber.
8. Frazier *et al.*, p. 33.
9. Hinsie, L. E. & Campbell, R. J. (1960) *Psychiatric Dictionary 3rd edn* p. 135 New York: Oxford University Press.
10. Hinsie & Campbell (1970) p. 147.

Conative. 'Pertains to the basic strivings of an individual as expressed in his behaviour and actions; volitional as contrasted with cognitive.'[1]

Concentration. See Attention.

Conflict. 'A mental struggle that arises from the simultaneous operation of opposing impulses, drives, or external (environmental) or internal drives; termed intrapsychic when the conflict is between forces within the personality, extrapsychic when it is between the self and the environment.'[2]

Confrontation. 'Act of letting a person know where one stands in relationship to him, what one is experiencing, and how one perceives him.'[3]

Confusion. 'Disturbed orientation in respect to time, place, or person.'[4] See Mental status.

Conscious. 'That part of the mind or mental functioning of which the content is subject to awareness or known to the person. In neurology: awake, alert. Contrast with unconscious.'[5]

Contraindication. 'A reason for not doing something; more specifically, a feature or complication of a condition that countermands the use of a therapeutic agent that might otherwise be applied.'[6]

Conversation. 'Oral exchange of sentiments, observations, opinions, ideas: colloquial discourse.'[7]

Cooperation. 'To act or work together with another or others for a common purpose; a joint effort or operation.'[8]

Coordination. 'Harmonious action, as of muscles.'[9]

Creativity. The 'ability to produce something new. Silvano Arieti describes creativity as the tertiary process, a balanced continuation of primary and secondary processes, whereby materials from the id are used in the service of the ego.'[10]

Debility. 'Weakness.'[11]

Decision. 'The act of making up one's mind; the act of forming an opinion or deciding upon a course of action; a judgement or conclusion reached or given.'[12]

Defence mechanism. 'Unconscious intrapsychic processes serving to provide relief from emotional conflict and anxiety. Conscious efforts are frequently made for the same reasons, but true defence mechanisms are unconscious. Some common defence mechanisms are: compensation, conversion, denial, displacement, dissociation, idealization, identification, incorporation, introjection, projection, rationalization, reaction

---

1. Frazier *et al.*, p. 35.
2. Ibid., p. 36
3. Freedman *et al.* (1972) p. 759.
4. Frazier *et al.*, p. 36.
5. Ibid.
6. Hinsie & Campbell (1970) p. 161.
7. Webster (1971) p. 498.
8. Webster (1968) p. 325.
9. Faber, p. 106.
10. Freedman *et al.* (1972) p. 761.
11. Faber, p. 118.
12. Webster (1968) p. 380.

formation, regression, sublimation, substitution, symbolization, un-doing.'[1] See Mental mechanism.

Delusion. 'A firm, fixed idea not amenable to rational explanation. Main-tained against logical argument despite objective contradictory evidence. Common delusions include:

delusions of grandeur: exaggerated ideas of one's importance or identity.

delusions of persecution: ideas that one has been singled out for perse-cution. See also Paranoia.

delusions of reference: incorrect assumption that certain casual or unrelated events or the behaviour of others apply to oneself.'[2]

Dependency. 'This generally means "a form of behaviour which suggests inability to make decisions; marked inclination to lean on others for advice, guidance, support, etc." (Hamilton, G. (1930) *A Medical Social Terminology* New York: Presbyterian Hospital.'[3]

Depression. In psychiatry, a morbid state characterized by a marked sad-ness, low self-esteem and self-reproach, psychomotor retardation, withdrawal and at times by the desire to die. It should be differentiated from grief which is realistic and proportionate to what has been lost. Depression may be a symptom of any psychiatric disorder or may con-stitute it's principal manifestation.

Dialogue. 'A conversation between two or more persons.'[4] Compare with Monologue.

Disappointment. 'The state or condition of being disappointed: failure of expectation or hope.'[5]

Discuss, to. 'To examine, to talk about; take up in conversation or in a dis-course; consider and argue the pros and cons of.

Syn: to discuss implies talking about something in a deliberate fashion, with varying opinions offered constructively and usually amicably.'[6]

Discussion. 'Consideration of a question in open, usually informal debate.'[7]

Distractibility. 'Inability to focus one's attention.'[8]

Dominance. In psychiatry, 'an individual's disposition to play a prominent or controlling role in his interaction with others.'[9]

Ego. 'In psychoanalytic theory . . . the ego represents the sum of certain mental mechanisms, such as perception and memory, and specific defence mechanisms. The ego serves to mediate between the demands of primitive instinctual drives (the id), of internalized parental and social prohibitions (the superego), and of reality. The compromises between these forces achieved by the ego tend to resolve intrapsychic conflict and serve as an adaptive and executive function.'[10]

Ego boundary. 'A concept introduced by *Federn* to refer to "the peripheral sense organ of the ego." The ego boundary discriminates what is real

---

1. Frazier *et al.*, p. 40.
2. Frazier *et al.*, p. 41.
3. Hinsie & Campbell (1970) p. 199.
4. Webster (1971) p. 622.
5. Ibid., p. 643.
6. Webster (1968) p. 418.
7. Webster (1971) p. 648.
8. Freedman *et al.* (1972) p. 763.
9. Frazier *et al.*, p. 45.
10. Frazier *et al.*, p. 48.

from what is unreal. There are two main ego boundaries, the inner and the outer.'[1] The inner boundary prevents the entrance of repressed material into the conscious, while the outer one is the boundary toward stimuli of the external world.

Egocentric. 'Refers to a person who is self-centred, preoccupied with his own needs, selfish and lacking interest in others.'[2]

Ego-strength. 'The effectiveness with which the ego discharges its various functions. A strong ego will not only mediate between id, superego, and reality and integrate these functions, but further it will do so with enough flexibility so that energy will remain for reactivity and other needs. This is in contrast to the rigid personality in which ego functions are maintained, but only at the cost of impoverishment of the personality.'[3]

Emotion. 'A feeling such as fear, anger, grief, joy or love which may not always be conscious.'[4] See also Affect and Feeling.

Empathy. 'An objective and insightful awareness of the feelings, emotions, and behaviour of another person, their meaning and significance; usually subjective and noncritical. Contrast with Sympathy.'[5]

Evaluate. 'To examine and judge concerning the worth, quality, significance, amount, degree or condition of.'[6]

Evaluation. 'The act or result of evaluating,'[7] See Assessment.

Exercise. 'Repetition of an act in order to learn it or increase skill.'[8]

Experiencing. 'Feeling emotions and feelings as opposed to thinking; being involved in what is happening, rather than standing back at a distance and theorizing.'[9]

Extemporaneous. 'Impromptu; performed on the spur of the moment.'[10]

Extrapsychic. See Conflict.

Extraversion. 'A state in which attention and energies are largely directed outward from the self.'[11] Contrast with Introversion.

Eye-contact. Describes the mutual glances that occur between people during social interaction. The degree of eye-contact depends on such factors as whether the participants like one another, how involved they are in their discussion, the nature of the topic under discussion and their physical position in relation to one another. The degree of eye-contact may also follow a cultural pattern that presumes touching, no touch, interpersonal spacing and the way people orient their bodies.

Feedback. 'Communication to the sender of the effect his original message had on those to whom it was relayed. Feedback may alter or re-enforce

---

1. Hinsie & Campbell (1960) p. 101.
2. Freedman *et al.* (1972) p. 765.
3. Hinsie & Campbell (1970) p. 256.
4. Frazier *et al.*, p. 50.
5. Ibid., p. 51.
6. Webster (1971) p. 786.
7. Ibid.
8. Wolman, Benjamin I. (1973) *Dictionary of Behavioural Science* p. 131 New York: Litton Educational Publishing.
9. Freedman *et al.* (1976) p. 1300.
10. Webster (1971) p. 804.
11. Frazier *et al.*, p. 54.

the original idea; it is a function that is basic to correction and self-correction.'[1]

Feeling. '(1) Subjective description for awareness of bodily (neutral) states that cannot be reliably referred to environmental wants.

(2) Tactile sensation.

(3) Awareness of something, i.e., feeling of being accepted.

(4) Emotion, e.g., feeling happy, sad, angry, etc.'[2]

Flight of ideas. 'Verbal skipping from one idea to another. The ideas appear to be continuous but are fragmentary and determined by chance or temporal associations. Sometimes seen in manic-depressive psychosis.'[3]

Focus. 'A central point: a point of concentration or of emanation: to cause to be concentrated.'[4]

Gesture. This refers to any action or posture intended to express an idea or feeling or to enforce or emphasize an argument, assertion or opinion. It is a form of nonverbal communication using the hands and to a lesser extent the head and feet.

Goal. 'In sociology... the term goal denotes any change in a situation which a person or group intends to bring about through his or its action.'[5] Synonyms of goal are end, objective and purpose.

Group. 'A number of objects or individuals capable of being regarded as a collective unit, or having a unity of its own; a pattern or configuration of objects perceived as a whole or Gestalt.'[6]

Group cohesion. 'Effect of the mutual bonds between members of a group as a result of their concentrated effort for a common interest and purpose. Until cohesiveness is achieved, the group cannot concentrate its full energy on a common task.'[7]

Group dynamics. This 'denotes the study of (a) the structure and functioning of groups, notably the psychological aspects of "small groups", with especial reference to the changing pattern of intra-group adjustment, tension, conflict and cohesion; and (b) the shifts in relationships of one group with another.'[8]

Group pressure. 'Demand by group members that individual members submit and conform to group standards, values and behaviour.'[9]

Hallucination. 'A false sensory perception in the absence of an actual external stimulus. May be induced by emotional and other factors such as drugs, alcohol and stress. May occur in any of the senses.'[10]

Honesty. 'In therapy, honesty is a value manifested by the ability to communicate one's immediate experience, including inconsistent, conflicting or ambivalent feelings and perceptions.'[11]

---

1. Hinsie & Campbell (1970) p. 298.
2. Wolman, p. 143.
3. Frazier *et al.*, p. 56.
4. Webster (1971) p. 881.
5. Gould, J. & Kolb, W. L. (Eds.) (1964) *A Dictionary of the Social Sciences* p. 290 London: Tavistock.
6. Drever, p. 112.
7. Freedman *et al.* (1972) p. 770.
8. Gould & Kolb, p. 297.
9. Freedman *et al.* (1972) p. 770.
10. Frazier *et el.*, p. 61.
11. Freedman *et al.* (1972) p. 771.

Hyperactive. 'Excessively or abnormally active.'[1]

Id. 'In Freudian theory, that part of the personality structure which harbours the unconscious instinctual desires and strivings of the individual.'[2] See Ego and Superego.

Identity-crisis. 'A loss of the sense of sameness and historical continuity of one's self, and inability to accept or adopt the role the subject perceives as being expected of him by society; often expressed by isolation, withdrawal, extremism, rebelliousness, and negativity, and typically triggered by a combination of sudden increase in the strength of instinctual drives in a milieu of rapid social evolution and technological change.'[3]

Improvisation. 'In psychodrama, the acting out of problems without prior preparation;'[4] to perform or act on the spur of the moment without any preparation.

Impulse. 'A psychic striving; usually refers to an instinctual urge.'[5]

Inadequate. 'Lacking the capacity for psychological maturity: unable to make adequate social adjustment.'[6]

Indecision. 'Inability or failure to arrive at a decision; wavering between two or more courses of action.'[7]

Individual. 'Jung defines the psychological individual as a "unique being". The psychological individual is characterized by it's peculiar, and in certain respects, unique psychology.'[8]

Individuation. 'The process of forming and specializing the individual nature; in particular, it is the development of the psychological individual as a differentiated being from the general, collective psychology.'[9]

Inhibition. 'In psychiatry, an unconscious defence against forbidden instinctual drives; it may interfere with or restrict specific activities or general patterns of behaviour.'[10]

Initiation. 'The process of beginning an activity or movement.'[11]

Insight. 'Self-understanding. The extent of the individual's understanding of the origin, nature, and mechanisms of his attitudes and behaviour. More superficially, recognition by a patient that he is ill.'[12] 'Most therapists distinguish two types: (1) intellectual insight: knowledge and awareness without any change of maladaptive behaviour; (2) emotional or visceral insight: awareness, knowledge, and understanding of one's own maladaptive behaviour, leading to positive changes in personality and behaviour.'[13]

---

1. Faber, p. 213.
2. Frazier *et al.*, p. 64.
3. Ibid., p. 65.
4. Freedman *et al.*, (1976) p. 1308.
5. Frazier *et al.*, p. 66.
6. Webster (1971) p. 1139.
7. Ibid., p. 1146.
8. Hinsie & Campbell (1970) p. 390.
9. Hinsie & Campbell (1970) p. 390.
10. Frazier *et al.*, p. 89.
11. Drever, p. 138.
12. Frazier, *et al.*, p. 89.
13. Freedman *et al.* (1976) p. 1309.

Intelligence. 'According to Thorndike, there are three distinct types of intelligence; abstract, mechanical and social. The capacity to understand and manage abstract ideas and symbols constitutes abstract intelligence; the ability to understand, invent and manage mechanisms comprises mechanical intelligence; and the capacity to act reasonably and wisely as regards human relations and social affairs constitutes social intelligence.'[1]

Intelligence quotient. 'The ratio of the subject's intelligence (determined by mental measures) to so-called average or normal intelligence for his age. The most common method for determining the I.Q. is to divide the assigned mental age by the chronological age.'[2]

Inter- (Lat.). 'Prefix meaning "between" or "among".'[3]

Interact. 'To act on each other; act reciprocally.'[4]

Interaction. See Social interaction and Nonverbal interaction.

Interpersonal relations. 'Refers to everything that "goes on" between one person and another (or others) by way of perception, evaluation, understanding and mode of reaction.'[5]

Interpersonal skill. 'Ability of a person in relationship with others to express his feelings appropriately, to be socially responsive, to change and influence, and to work and create.'[6] See Socialization.

Intra- (Lat.). 'Prefix meaning "within" or "inside".'[7]

Intrapsychic. See Conflict.

Introversion. 'Preoccupation with oneself and accompanying reduction of interest in the outside world; the reverse of extraversion.'[8]

Isolation. 'A defence mechanism, operating unconsciously, in which an unacceptable impulse, idea, or act is separated from it's original memory source, thereby removing the emotional charge associated with the original memory.'[9] 'Isolation may (also) be defined as a lack of family and social contacts' and as such it 'has to be distinguished from loneliness, although the two often co-exist.'[10]

Judgement. 'Mental act of comparing or evaluating choices within the framework of a given set of values for the purpose of selecting a course of action. Judgement is said to be intact if the course of action chosen is consistent with reality. Judgement is said to be impaired if the chosen course of action is not consistent with reality.'[11]

Kinesics (kinesiology). 'The study of body movement as part of the process of communication; sociological analysis of interactional activity.'[12]

---

1. Hinsie & Campbell (1970) p. 406.
2. Ibid., p. 640.
3. Webster (1968) p. 761.
4. Ibid.
5. Gould & Kolb, p. 350.
6. Freedman *et al.* (1976) p. 1310.
7. Drever, p. 144.
8. Frazier *et al.*, p. 90.
9. Ibid.
10. Leigh, D., Pare, C. M. B. & Marks, J. (Eds.) (1977) *A Concise Encyclopaedia of Psychiatry* p. 207 Baltimore: University Park Press.
11. Freedman *et al.* (1976) p. 1311.
12. Frazier *et al.*, p. 92.

Kinesics includes the study of body posture, movement and facial expression.

Labile. 'Unstable, characterized by rapidly changing emotions.'[1]

Leadership' 'Leadership "may be broadly defined as the relation between an individual and a group built around some common interest and behaving in a manner directed or determined by him." (Schmidt, R. (1933) *Leadership; Encyclopaedia of the Social Sciences,* Vol. 9, p. 282. New York: Macmillan).'[2]

Leadership role. 'Stance adopted by the therapist in conducting a group. There are three main leadership roles: authoritarian, democratic, and laissez-faire. Any group – social, therapeutic, training or task oriented – is primarily influenced by the role practised by the leader.'[3]

Mania. 'A mood disorder characterized by excessive elation, hyperactivity, agitation, and accelerated thinking and speaking, sometimes manifested in flight of ideas. Mania is seen most frequently as one of the two major forms of manic-depressive psychosis.'[4]

Manic-depressive psychosis. 'A major affective disorder characterized by severe mood swings and a tendency to remission and recurrence. It is divided into the following three sub-groups:

circular type: an illness distinguished by at least one depressive episode and a manic episode.

depressed type: a depressive illness consisting exclusively of depressive episodes characterized by severely depressed mood and by motor and mental retardation that may progress to stupor.

manic type: an illness consisting of manic episodes characterized by excessive elation, irritability, talkativeness, flight of ideas, and accelerated speech and motor activity.'[5]

See also Depression.

Medium, media. 'A condition, atmosphere, or environment in which something may function or flourish: the material or technical means for artistic expression (as paint, canvas . . . or musical form).'[6]

Memory. 'Ability to revive past sensory impressions, experiences and learned ideas. Memory includes three basic mental processes:

registration: the ability to perceive, recognize and establish information in the central nervous system;

retention: the ability to retain registered information; and

recall: the ability to retrieve stored information at will.'[7]

Mental disorder. 'Any psychiatric illness or disease included in the World Health Organization's *International Classification of Diseases.*'[8]

---

1. Freedman *et al.* (1976) p. 1312.
2. Hinsie & Campbell (1970) p. 429.
3. Freedman *et al.* (1972) p. 777.
4. Frazier *et al.*, p. 97.
5. Ibid.
6. Webster (1971) p. 1403.
7. Freedman *et al.* (1972) p. 779.
8. Frazier *et al.*, p. 99.

Mental mechanism. 'A generic term for a variety of psychic processes that are functions of the ego and largely unconscious. Includes perception, memory, thinking and defence mechanisms.'[1]

Mental status. 'The level and style of functioning of the psyche, used in its broadest sense to include intellectual functioning as well as the emotional, attitudinal, psychological and personality aspects of the subject; in clinical psychiatry, the term is commonly used to refer to the results of the examination of the patient's mental state. Such an examination ordinarily aims to achieve one or more of the following:

(1) evaluation and assessment of any psychiatric condition present including provisional diagnosis and prognosis, determination of degree of impairment, suitability for treatment, and indications for particular types of therapeutic intervention;

(2) formulation of the personality structure of the subject, which may suggest the historical and developmental antecedents of whatever psychiatric condition exists;

(3) estimate of the ability and willingness of the subject to participate appropriately in the treatment regimen considered desirable for him. The mental status is reported in a series of narrative statements describing such things as: affect, speech, thought content, perceptions, and cognitive functions, including orientation.'[2]

Mime. 'The art of creating and portraying a character or of narration by body movement (as by realistic and symbolic gestures); (to) play a part with mimic gesture and action usually without words.'[3]

Monologue. 'A long speech uttered by one person while in company with others.'[4] Contrast with Dialogue.

Mood. The 'feeling tone that is experienced by a person internally. Mood does not include the external expression of the internal feeling tone.'[5] See also Affect.

Motivation. The 'force that pushes a person to act to satisfy a need. It implies an incentive or desire that influences the will and causes the person to act.'[6]

Negative feelings. In psychiatry these refer to unfriendly or hostile feelings.

Neologism. 'Neologisms are part of the speech disturbance which reflects the disordered thoughts of schizophrenics. They are words of the patient's own making, often condensations of other words and having a special meaning for the patient.'[7]

Neurosis (psychoneurosis). 'An emotional maladaptation arising from an unresolved unconscious conflict. The anxiety is either felt directly or modified by various psychological mechanisms to produce other, subjectively distressing symptoms. The neuroses are usually considered less severe than the psychoses (although not always less disabling) because

1. Frazier *et al.*, p. 99.
2. Frazier *et al.* p. 100.
3. Webster (1971) p. 1436.
4. Ibid., p. 1463.
5. Freedman *et al.* (1976) p. 1316.
6. Freedman *et al.* (1976) p. 1317.
7. Leigh *et al.*, p. 254.

they manifest neither gross personality disorganization nor gross distortion or misinterpretation of external reality. The neuroses are classified according to predominating symptoms. The common neuroses are: anxiety neurosis, depersonalization neurosis, depressive neurosis, hypochondriacal neurosis, hysterical neurosis (a) conversion type, or (b) dissociative type, neurasthenic neurosis, obsessive compulsive neurosis, phobic neurosis.'[1]

Nonverbal interaction. Technique used without the aid of words in groups to promote communication and intimacy and to by-pass verbal defences. Many exercises of this sort are carried out in complete silence; in others the participants emit grunts, groans, yells, cries or sighs. Gestalt therapy pays particular attention to nonverbal expression.

Objective. 'Expressing or involving the use of facts without distortion by personal feelings or prejudices.'[2]

Observation. 'An act of recognizing and noting some fact or occurrence.'[3]

Obsessive-compulsive (psycho)neurosis. 'A type of psychoneurosis characterized by disturbing, unwanted, anxiety-provoking, intruding thoughts or ideas, and repetitive impulses to perform acts (ceremonials, counting, hand-washing, etc.) which may be considered abnormal, undesirable or distasteful to the patient.'[4]

Occupational therapy. 'An adjunctive therapy that utilizes purposeful activities as a means of altering the course of illness. The patient's relationship to staff personnel and to other patients in the occupational therapy setting is often more therapeutic than the activity itself.'[5]

Opinion. 'A belief not based on absolute certainty or positive knowledge but on what seems true, valid or probable to one's own mind.'[6]

Optimum. 'The amount or degree of something that is most favourable to some end.'[7]

Orientation. 'Awareness of one's self in relation to time, place and person.'[8]

Overinclusion. 'Overinclusive thinking is one aspect of thought disorder in acute schizophrenia. There is an inability to preserve conceptual boundaries, so that ideas only distinctly related to a particular concept become included in that concept. The "wooliness" of schizophrenic thought is a result of this type of thought disorder.'[9]

Paranoid. 'An adjective applied to individuals who are overly suspicious.'[10]

Participation. 'The action or state of taking part with others in an activity.'[11] See also Activity.

Parkinsonism. See Tremor.

1. Frazier *et al.*, p. 106.
2. Webster (1971) p. 1556.
3. Webster (1971) p. 1558.
4. Hinsie & Campbell (1970) p. 519.
5. Frazier *et al.*, p. 108.
6. Webster (1968) p. 1028.
7. Ibid. (1971) p. 1585.
8. Frazier *et al.*, p. 111.
9. Leigh *et al.*, p. 268.
10. Frazier *et al.*, p. 112.
11. Webster (1971) p. 1646.

Passivity. 'One of the several modalities of adaptation. For example, it is possible for the organism to adapt itself to it's environment by going either forward to meet it or backward to escape it. The first procedure would be termed the modality of activity in adaptive behaviour, while the latter would be termed the modality of passivity.'[1]

Patient. 'A sick person.'[2]

Perception. 'Mental processes by which data – intellectual, sensory and emotional – are organized meaningfully. Through perception a person makes sense out of the many stimuli that bombard him. It is one of the many ego functions.'[3]

Perceptual expansion. 'Development of one's ability to recognize and interpret the meaning of sensory stimuli through associations with past experiences with similar stimuli. Perceptual expansion through the relaxation of defences is one of the goals of both individual and group therapy.'[4]

Personality. 'The characteristic way in which a person behaves; the ingrained pattern of behaviour that each person evolves, both consciously and unconsciously, as his style of life or way of being in adapting to his environment.'[5] See Personality disorders.

Personality disorders. 'A group of mental disorders characterized by deeply ingrained maladaptive patterns of behaviour, generally life-long in duration and consequently often recognizable by the time of adolescence or earlier. Affecting primarily the personality of the individual they are different in quality from neurosis and psychosis.'[6]

Philosophy. 'A critical examination of the grounds for fundamental beliefs and an analysis of the basic concepts employed in the expression of such beliefs.'[7]

Positive feelings. In psychiatry these refer to warm, friendly feelings as opposed to negative hostile feelings.

Poverty of ideas. Identified as a lack of spontaneous thoughts, ideas and associations. It is a psychiatric term describing a form of thought disorder often seen in schizophrenia.

Problem. 'An unsettled matter demanding solution or decision and requiring . . . considerable thought or skill for its proper solution or decision: something that is a source of perplexity or worry.'[8]

Problem oriented medical record. 'A simple conceptual framework to expedite and improve the medical record. The record is structured to contain four logical sequenced sections. (1) the data base, (2) the problem list, (3) plans, and (4) follow-up. The data base provides the information required for each patient regardless of diagnosis or presenting problems. The problem list is the list of the numbered problems characterizing the patient to be treated. The plans specify what is to be done with regard to each problem, including what further needs to be done to identify and

1. Hinsie & Campbell (1970) p. 548.
2. Faber, p. 337.
3. Freedman *et al.* (1976) p. 1320.
4. Ibid.
5. Frazier *et al.*, p. 115.
6. Ibid., p. 116
7. Webster (1971) p. 1698.
8. Ibid., p. 1807.

delineate the problem, what treatments are to be enacted for each problem and what education of the patient and family is to be conducted regarding his problems. Plans are specified for each problem separately. Follow-up includes progress notes and often flow sheets. Progress notes are titled by problem title and numbered according to their number on the problem list. Each progress note is subdivided into a data section (differentiated by data source – subjective and objective), assessments of the data entered concerning the problem, and plans for the problem as it has been assessed.'[1]

Projection. 'Unconscious defence mechanism in which a person attributes to another the ideas, thoughts, feelings, and impulses that are part of his inner perceptions but that are unacceptable to him. Projection protects the person from anxiety arising from an inner conflict. By externalizing whatever is unacceptable, the person deals with it as a situation apart from himself.'[2]

Projective techniques. 'Methods used to discover an individual's attitudes, motivations, defensive manoeuvres and characteristic ways of responding through analysis of their responses to unstructured, ambiguous stimuli.'[3] As a group treatment procedure they make use of the spontaneous creative work of each patient. For example, group members make and analyse drawings, which in turn often express their underlying emotional problems.

Psychiatry. 'The medical science that deals with the origin, diagnosis, prevention and treatment of mental disorders.'[4]

Psychomotor. 'Relating to voluntary movement.'[5]

Psychomotor retardation. 'A generalized "retardation" of physical and emotional reactions.'[6]

Psychosis. 'A major mental disorder of organic or emotional origin in which the individual's ability to think, respond emotionally, remember, communicate, interpret reality, and behave appropriately is sufficiently impaired so as to interfere grossly with his capacity to meet the ordinary demands of life. Often characterized by regressive behaviour, inappropriate mood, diminished impulse control, and such abnormal mental content as delusions and hallucinations. The term is applicable to conditions having a wide range of severity and duration.'[7] See Schizophrenia, Manic-depressive psychosis, Depression and Reality testing.

Purpose. See Goal.

Reaction(s). 'Counter-action; response to a stimulus.'[8]

Reality. 'The totality of objective things and factual events. Reality includes everything that is perceived by a person's special senses and is validated by other people.'[9]

1. Frazier *et al.*, p. 122.
2. Freedman *et al.* (1976) p. 1322.
3. Wolman, p. 291.
4. Frazier *et al.*, p. 124.
5. Faber, p. 368.
6. Frazier *et al.*, p. 126.
7. Ibid., p. 127.
8. Hinsie & Campbell (1970) p. 645.
9. Freedman *et al.* (1976) p. 1325.

Reality, contact with. See Reality testing.

Reality testing. A 'fundamental ego function that consists of objective evaluation and judgement of the world outside the self. By interacting with his animate and inanimate environment, a person tests its real nature, as well as his own relation to it. How the person evaluates reality and his attitudes towards it are determined by early experiences with significant persons in his life.'[1] The ability to evaluate the external world objectively and differentiate adequately between it and the internal world, between self and non-self. Falsification of reality, as with massive denial or projection, indicates a severe disturbance of ego functioning and/or the perceptual and memory processes upon which it is partly based.'[2] See also Ego and Psychosis.

Reasoning. 'A process of thinking involving inference, or of solving problems by employing general principles.'[3]

Recall. 'The process of bringing memory into consciousness.' In psychiatry, 'recall is often used to refer to the recollection of facts and events in the immediate past.'[4] See Memory.

Recognition. 'Perceiving (or recalling) an object, accompanied by a feeling of familiarity, or the conviction that the same object has been perceived before.'[5] 'To acknowledge as worthy of appreciation or approval.'[6]

Relatedness. 'The interrelation between two or more people who reciprocally influence each other, as patient-therapist, mother-child, etc. Normal relatedness is based on security in interpersonal relations and in large part is a result of early childhood experiences.'[7]

Relatedness, functional. 'The arrangement of objects that are organically and dynamically related to each other; for example, placing woodworking tools near the woodworking bench and nails and other objects involved in woodworking nearby; placing drawing paper near crayons and paints in the proximity of an easel.'[8]

Relaxation. 'Diminution of tension.'[9]

Repression. 'A defence mechanism, operating unconsciously, that banishes unacceptable ideas, affects or impulses from consciousness, or that keeps out of consciousness what has never been conscious. Although not subject to voluntary recall, the repressed material may emerge in disguised form. Often confused with the conscious mechanism of suppression.'[10]

Resistance. 'The individual's conscious or unconscious psychological defence against bringing repressed (unconscious) thoughts to light.'[11] See Mental Mechanism.

---

1. Freedman *et al.* (1976) p. 1325.
2. Frazier *et al.*, p. 131.
3. Drever, p. 241.
4. Frazier *et al.*, p. 131.
5. Drever, p. 242.
6. Webster (1968) p. 1214.
7. Hinsie & Campbell (1970) p. 658.
8. Ibid.
9. Faber, p. 379.
10. Frazier *et al.*, p. 133.
11. Ibid.

Retardation. 'Slowness or backwardness of intellectual development; when used in this sense, mental retardation is the usual phrase. Slowness of response, a slowing down of thinking and/or a decrease in psychomotor activity; in this later sense, the term psychomotor retardation is the appropriate phrase. Psychomotor retardation is characteristic of clinical depressions.'[1]

Risk. 'The chance of incurring damage or a loss of some kind (physical, psychological, military, political, economic, etc.).'[2] In psychiatry the term is usually used to mean 'taking a chance' or 'exposing oneself to the chance of . . .'.

Role. 'Pattern of behaviour that a person takes. It has its roots in childhood and is influenced by significant people with whom the person had primary relationships. When the behaviour pattern conforms with the expectations and demands of other people, it is said to be a complementary role. If it does not conform with the demands and expectations of others, it is known as a noncomplementary role.'[3]

Role-playing. 'Psychodrama technique in which a person is trained to function more effectively in his reality roles, such as employer, employee, student and instructor.'[4]

Schizophrenia. 'A large group of disorders, usually of psychotic proportion, manifested by characteristic disturbances of thought, mood and behaviour. Thought disturbances are marked by alterations of concept formation that may lead to misinterpretation of reality and sometimes to delusions and hallucinations. Mood changes include ambivalence, constriction, inappropriateness, and loss of empathy with others. Behaviour may be withdrawn, regressive, and bizarre.'[5]

Sedentary. (1.) Used in sitting. (2.) Related to the habit of sitting.'[6]

Self-analysis. 'Investigation of one's own psychic components.'[7]

Self-assertion. 'The act of demanding recognition for oneself or of asserting or insisting upon one's rights, claims, etc.'[8]

Self-awareness. 'Sense of knowing what one is experiencing; for example, realizing that one has responded with anger to another group member as a substitute for the anxiety left when he attacked a vital part of one's self-concept. Self-awareness is a major goal of all therapy, individual or group.'[9]

Self-conception. An individual's self-conception is his view of himself. Self-conception is the equivalent to the self, if the latter is defined as 'the individual as perceived by that individual in a socially determined frame of reference'. In addition to a view of self, self-conception includes notions of one's interests and aversions, a conception of one's goals and success

1. Hinsie & Campbell (1970) p. 665.
2. Gould & Kolb, p. 605.
3. Freedman *et al.* (1976) p. 1327.
4. Ibid.
5. Frazier *et al.*, p. 134.
6. Faber, p. 396.
7. Freedman *et al.* (1976) p. 1328.
8. Webster (1968) p. 1321.
9. Freedman *et al.* (1976) p. 1328.

in achieving them, a picture of the ideological frame of reference through which one views oneself and other objects and some knowledge of self-evaluation.

Self-confidence. 'The quality of being self-confident; belief in or reliance on oneself or one's abilities.'[1]

Self-consciousness. 'Awareness of one's own existence, thoughts and actions; popularly embarrassment or shyness.'[2]

Self-esteem. 'Belief in oneself; self-respect.'[3] 'A state of being on good terms with one's superego. Pathological loss of self-esteem is characteristic of clinical depression.'[4]

Self-expression. 'The expression of one's own personality or emotions, especially through some art form.'[5]

Self-respect. 'A proper respect for oneself, one's character and one's behaviour.'[6] See Self-esteem.

Sensory. 'Relating to or conducting sensation.'[7]

Social interaction. 'Denotes the reciprocal influencing of the acts of persons in groups, usually mediated through communication. This definition includes the interaction of a person with himself. It may be defined operationally as what happens when people come into contact (not necessarily physical contact) and a modification of behaviour takes place.'[8]

Social isolation. See Isolation.

Socialization. The process by which society integrates the individual and the way in which the individual learns to become a functioning member of that society. 'In occupational therapy the term is applied to the development (in a patient) of those tendencies which induce him to be companionable and inclined to seek and mingle easily with a group.'[9]

Spontaneous. 'Of personal actions: Arising or proceeding entirely from natural impulse; without any external stimulus or constraint; voluntary and of one's own accord.'[10]

Stimulation. See Activation.

Subjective. 'Arising from within or belonging strictly to the individual . . .: arising out of or identified by means of an individual's attention to or awareness of his own states and processes.'[11]

Submission. 'The act of yielding to others; a type of behaviour on the part of an individual manifesting a tendency to submit to the dominance of others.'[12]

Superego. 'In psychoanalytic theory, that part of the personality structure associated with ethics, standards and self-criticism. It is formed by the

1. Webster (1968) p. 1322.
2. Drever, p. 262.
3. Webster (1968) p. 1322.
4. Hinsie & Campbell (1960) p. 670.
5. Webster (1968) p. 1322.
6. Ibid., p. 1323.
7. Faber, p. 397.
8. Gould & Kolb, p. 657.
9. Hinsie & Campbell (1960) p. 681.
10. *A New English Dictionary, Vol IX. Part I. SI–ST* (1919) Murray, J. A. H., Bradley, H., Craigie, W. A. & Onions, C. T. (Eds.) p. 659 Oxford: Clarendon Press.
11. Webster (1971) p. 2275.
12. Drever, p. 286.

infant's identification with important and esteemed persons in his early life, particularly parents. The supposed or actual wishes of these significant persons are taken over as part of the child's own personal standards to help form the conscience.'[1] See Ego and Id.

Support, to. 'To actively promote the interests of . . .: to give assistance to.'[2]

Supportive psychotherapy. 'A type of psychotherapy that aims to reinforce a patient's defences and to help him suppress disturbing psychological material. Supportive psychotherapy utilizes such measures as inspiration, reassurance, suggestion, persuasion, counselling and re-education. It avoids probing the patient's emotional conflicts in depth.'[3]

Suppression. 'The conscious effort to control and conceal unacceptable impulses, thoughts, feelings, or acts.'[4]

Symbolization. 'An unconscious mental process operating by association and based on similarity and abstract representation whereby one object or idea comes to stand for another through some part, quality or aspect which the two have in common. The symbol carries in more or less disguised form the emotional feelings vested in the initial object or idea.'[5]

Sympathy. 'Compassion for another's grief or loss. To be differentiated from empathy.'[6]

Tactile. 'Relating to the sense of touch.'[7]

Tension. 'An unpleasant alteration of affect characterized by a strenuous increase in mental and physical activity.'[8]

Theatre game. A simple, structured exercise often used by actors to improve their abilities to think quickly, to be spontaneous, to improvise, to speak clearly, to trust others, to work in cooperation with others, to concentrate and to be decisive. The emphasis in a theatre game is upon clear, direct communication whether it be verbal or nonverbal, and if it is used appropriately and in conjuction with other theatre games it can offer an excellent opportunity to practise, improve or change social behaviour in an enjoyable and accepting atmosphere.

Therapeutic. 'Of or relating to the treatment of disease or disorders by remedial agents or methods.'[9]

Thinking. 'Any course or train of ideas; in the narrower and stricter sense, a course of ideas initiated by a problem.'[10]

Thinking, abstract. 'Thinking which is characterized by the use of abstractions and generalizations.'[11]

Thinking, concrete. The antithesis of abstract thinking. Concrete thinking is often associated with impairment of the frontal lobes. It is characterized by 'an inability to detach the ego from the inner and outer sphere of

---

1. Frazier *et al.*, p. 143.
2. Webster (1971) p. 2297.
3. Frazier *et al.*, p. 144.
4. Ibid.
5. Ibid.
6. Ibid.
7. Faber, p. 430.
8. Freedman *et al.* (1976) p. 1333.
9. Webster (1971) p. 2372.
10. Drever, p. 298.
11. Wolman, p. 386.

experience; an inability to concentrate on two tasks simultaneously; to integrate parts into a whole or to analyse a totality; and an inability to judge, reflect about or plan for the future.'[1]

Tremor. 'Shaking or trembling. A disorder of muscular tone in which the usual, normal, unappreciable tonic contractions of a muscle become exaggerated to the point of awareness. In general tremors can be classified into:

(1) coarse tremors, usually indicative of organic disease; included are –
   (a) passive or rest tremor, a tremor that occurs while the affected area is at rest, as the pill-rolling tremor of Parkinsonism;
   (b) action or intention tremor, which may be absent while the affected area is at rest and which is exaggerated by voluntary movement of the area, as the intention tremor of multiple sclerosis;
(2) fine tremors, often psychogenic although they may also be on a toxic basis (alcoholism, drug poisoning, hyperthyroidism, etc.);
(3) fasciculation, involuntary twitchings of a portion of a muscle; seen in fatigue, also in brain stem or anterior horn cell damage.'[2]

Trust, basic. 'S. Arieti (*Archives of General Psychiatry* 6, 112–122, 1962) emphasizes that basic trust is essential for the development of normal or satisfying relatedness.' 'Basic trust is an "atmospheric feeling" which predisposes one to expect "good things" and is a prerequisite to a normal development of self-esteem . . . .'[3]

Unconscious. That part of the mind or mental functioning of which the content is only rarely subject to awareness. It is the repository for data that have never been conscious (primary repression) or that may have become conscious briefly and later repressed (secondary repression).'[4]

Verbalization. 'In psychiatry, the state of being verbose or diffuse, commonly encountered in extreme degree in patients with the manic form of manic-depressive psychosis. In a more general sense, verbalization refers to the expression in words of thoughts, wishes, fantasies, or other psychic material which had previously been on a nonverbal level because of suppression or repression. "Verbalize" is often used in a pseudo-erudite way when "talk about" is meant.'[5]

Verbal technique. 'Any method of group or individual therapy in which words are used.'[6]

Videotape. 'A magnetic tape on which the electronic impulses of the video and audio portions of a television program can be recorded for later broadcasting.'[7]

1. Wolman, p. 386.
2. Hinsie & Campbell (1970) p. 785.
3. Hinsie & Campbell (1970) p. 658.
4. Frazier *et al.*, p. 149.
5. Hinsie & Campbell (1970) p. 803.
6. Freedman *et al.* (1972) p. 799.
7. Webster (1968) p. 1625.

Warm-up exercise. A technique, exercise or game of short duration used to promote an atmosphere in which a person can begin to look at specific problems in greater detail.

Withdrawal. 'The act of retracting, retiring, retreating or going away from. Withdrawal is used in psychiatry to refer to . . . the turning away from objective, external reality . . . the patient's retreat from society and interpersonal relationships into a world of his own.'[1] Often seen in schizophrenia and depression.

Word salad. 'A mixture of words and/or phrases which have no logical meaning. Commonly associated with schizophrenia.'[2]

REFERENCES

Curren, D., Partridge, M. & Storey, P. (1976) *Psychological Medicine: An Introduction to Psychiatry.* Edinburgh: Churchill Livingstone.

Freedman, A. M., Kaplan, H. I. & Sadock, B. J. (Eds.) (1975) *Comprehensive Textbook of Psychiatry.* Baltimore: Williams & Wilkins.

Freedman, A. M., Kaplan, H. I. & Sadock, B. J. (Eds.) (1976) *Modern Synopsis of Comprehensive Textbook of Psychiatry/II*, 2nd edn. Baltimore: Williams & Wilkins.

Harrison, Randall P. (1974) *Beyond Words: An Introduction to Nonverbal Communication.* New Jersey: Prentice-Hall.

Leigh, D., Pare, C. M. B., Marks, J. (Eds.) (1977) *A Concise Encyclopaedia of Psychiatry.* Baltimore: University Park Press.

1. Hinsie & Campbell (1970) p. 812.
2. Leigh *et al.*, p. 368.

Bibliography

This Bibliography offers some suggestions for supplementary reading; the books listed are taken from a wide variety of current publications. It invites you to both broaden your theoretical base and personal skills as well as sample a greater selection of nonverbal group techniques and their potential application.

Alberti, R. E. & Emmons, M. L. (1970) *Your Perfect Right: A Guide to Assertive Behaviour*. California: Impact.

Argyle, M. (1975) *Bodily Communication*. London: Methuen.

Argyle, M. (1967) *The Psychology of Interpersonal Behaviour*. Harmondsworth: Penguin.

Bellak, L. (1964) *Handbook of Community Psychiatry*. New York: Grune & Stratton.

Bower, S. A. & Bower, G. H. (1976) *Asserting Yourself: A Practical Guide for Positive Change*. Reading, Mass: Addison-Wesley.

Bry, A. (1975) *T. A. Games*. New York: Harper & Row.

Cumming, J. E. & Cumming, E. (1962) *Ego and Milieu; Theory & Practice of Environmental Therapy*. Chicago: Aldine.

Dodd, N. & Hickson, W. (Eds.) (1971) *Drama & Theatre in Education*. London: Heinemann.

Fast, J. (1970) *Body Language*. New York: Evans.

Glasser, W. (1965) *Reality Therapy; A New Approach to Psychiatry*. New York: Harper & Row.

Harrison, R. P. (1974) *Beyond Words: An Introduction to Nonverbal Communication*. New Jersey: Prentice-Hall.

Hay, D. & Rogers, D. J. (1974) *Moving Through the Universe in Bare Feet*. Chicago: Swallow Press.

Jongeward, D. & James, M. (1973) *Winning with People: Group Exercises in Transactional Analysis*. Reading, Mass: Addison-Wesley.

Kaplan, H. I. & Sadock, B. J. (Eds.) (1972) *Group Treatment of Mental Illness*. New York: Jason Aronson.

Kaplan, H. I. & Sadock, B. J. (1971) *Comprehensive Group Psychotherapy*. Baltimore: Williams & Wilkins.

Knapp, M. L. (1972) *Nonverbal Communication in Human Interaction*. New York: Holt, Rinehart & Winston.

Lader, M. H. (Ed.) (1975) *Studies of Schizophrenia*. Kent: Headley Brothers.

Lewis, H. R. & Streitfield, H. S. (1971) *Growth Games*. New York: Harcourt Brace Jovanovich.

Likach Marinoff, S. (1973) *When Words are Not Enough – Videotape*. Teaching Exceptional Children, Winter.

Lowen, A. (1971) *The Language of the Body*. New York: Collier Books.

Mahoney, S. C. (1967) *The Art of Helping People Effectively*. New York: Association Press.

Mehrabian, A. (1971) *Silent Messages*. Belmont, California: Wadsworth.

Merritt, R. E. (Jr.) & Walley, D. D. (1977) *The Group Leader's Handbook: Resources, Techniques and Survival Skills*. Illinois: Research Press.

Morris, K. T. & Cinnamon, K. M. (1975) *A Handbook of Nonverbal Group Exercises*. Springfield, Illinois: Thomas.

Otto, H. A. (1972) *Fantasy Encounter Games*. New York: Harper & Row.

Parry, R. (1975) *A Guide to Counselling and Basic Psychotherapy*. Edinburgh: Churchill Livingstone.

Pfeiffer, J. W. & Jones, J. E. (1973–75) *Handbook of Structured Experiences for Human Relations Training*. 6 Volumes. California: University Associates.

Phanidis, J. & Duncan, A. (1975) *Growing Inside Out*. Victoria, B.C.: Pioneer Publishing.

Rogers, C. R. & Stevens, B. (1967) *Person to Person; The Problem of Being Human*. Utah: Real People Press.

Schutz, W. C. (1967) *Joy; Expanding Human Awareness*. New York: Grove Press.

Smith, M. J. (1975) *When I Say No, I Feel Guilty*. London: Bantam.

Sprott, W. J. H. (1958) *Human Groups*. Harmondsworth: Penguin.

Stevens, J. O. (1971) *Awareness; Exploring, Experimenting, Experiencing*. Utah: Real People Press.

Watzlawick, P., Weakland, J. H. & Fisch, R. (1974) *Change: Principles of Problem Formation and Problem Resolution*. New York: Norton.

Way, B. (1967) *Development Through Drama*. Harlow: Longman.

Weitz, S. (Ed.). (1974) *Nonverbal Communication: Readings with Commentary*. New York: Oxford University Press.

Whitaker, D. S. & Lieberman, M. A. (1964) *Psychotherapy Through the Group Process*. New York: Atherton Press.

Index

Entries in italic are titles of exercises